FRANCE OBSERVED

Text by
Henri Gougaud and Colette Gouvion

Translated from the French
by Genevieve Westham

KAYE & WARD · LONDON

OXFORD UNIVERSITY PRESS · NEW YORK

First published in Great Britain 1977 by Kaye & Ward Ltd
21 New Street, London EC2M 4NT

First published in the USA 1977 by Oxford University Press Inc.
200 Madison Avenue, New York, NY 10016

ISBN 0 7182 1170 7 (Great Britain)

ISBN 0–19–519968–5 (USA)
Library of Congress Catalog Card Number 77–72704

Printed in France

CONTENTS

It is a land that can scarcely be beaten in the variety of atmospheres it evokes. Its diversity is such that it offers to the visitor echoes of many other European civilizations and cultures. And yet its own flavour is unique and unmistakable.

It is a land linked to the sea–four seas, each with its own special character. The North Sea, misty, nordic and dreamlike; the Channel; the warm, sun-drenched Mediterranean; and the Atlantic Ocean whose breakers roll on its western shores.

It is a land of mountains. Some of them are harsh and rugged, their icy summits and snowy slopes extending a challenge to human endurance. Others are older. Tamed and softened by age, their sharp contours are cloaked with woods and forests. All of them are pitted with lakes of limpid water.

It is a land where the countryside is rich and fertile,

verdant and peaceful, crossed by swift-flowing rivers and studded with gardens of roses and lilac.

It is a land of olive and oak, vineyard and cornfield, pastureland and moorland, bare rock and fertile soil, drought and humidity, heat and cold.

It is a land where every stage of human history has left its imprint: in prehistoric caves, in Roman remains, in the architecture of early Christendom, in Romanesque churches, Gothic cathedrals, Renaissance châteaux and 17th-century palaces.

It is a mosaic of towns and villages, a symphony of granite and pale stone, pink brick and blue slate, a symphony which takes its rhythm from a great city: Paris.

It is a land with a long history.

This land exists. It is a lesson in the art of living. It is called France. This book is an exploration of it.

H. G. and C. G.

Normandy

Along the Seine valley unfolds a leafy, verdant landscape, a patchwork of greenery which hangs as though suspended between the grey-green sea and the blue-grey sky. From the outskirts of Paris it stretches to the sea and then extends westwards along the coast to neighbouring Brittany. This is Normandy, a province whose name immediately conjures up in the mind a picture of apple-trees in blossom, fat cows grazing peacefully in lush pastureland, half-timbered houses squatting squarely in rolling meadows, rich creamy food, and a way of life deeply rooted in the fertile soil. This well-known image of Normandy is an accurate one, but it does not tell the whole story. It is a faithful description of the rich, fertile area known as the Pays d'Auge (literally "trough country") which extends from Caen in the west to the smart coastal resorts of Deauville and Trouville. But to be content with this idea of Normandy would be to leave out so much—the granite moorland landscape of the Cotentin peninsula, the sharply-defined contours of the hedge-enclosed pastureland known as the *bocage*, and the sheer, windswept cliffs of the Pays de Caux to the east. And, evocative though it is, this image of a Normandy rooted in the earth ignores the province's long seafaring tradition, which stretches back to the earliest days of its history and is still very much alive today.

The white cliffs of Etretat are as typical of Normandy as the green meadows of the hinterland. Erosion has gouged a massive door through one of them, a gloomy vaulted arch opening out to the boundless sea. Nearby rises a slender rocky pinnacle known as **L'Aiguille** (the needle). The wind and spray tirelessly carve and sharpen the rock; the heavy waves beat against its foot, and seagulls build their nests on its peak.

Here, more than 1,000 years ago, the history of Normandy began. When the Vikings (the Northmen or "Normans") slid their swift longboats through these gaps in the cliff, they had already sailed as far as America and plundered England and Ireland. Their very name struck terror into Europe from the Don to Byzantium, and from Spain to Italy. They sailed up the Seine as far as Paris, and Gaul trembled before them. The crafty King Charles, known as "the Simple", preferred to negotiate with the dreaded Northmen rather than attempt resistance. In 911 he signed a treaty with their leader, Rollo, at Saint-Clair-sur-Epte. By the terms of this treaty, Neustria, all the land between the Seine and Brittany, was handed over to the invaders, who in return became loyal vassals of the French king. The land granted to Rollo was to become known as the duchy of Normandy.

The cliffs at Etretat and the Aiguille rock.

Château-Gaillard.

And so the fierce sailors dropped anchor and settled down. Even today Normandy still bears many traces of their imprint. Many Normans have the reddish-blond hair, pale-blue eyes and tall, heavy silhouettes of their nordic ancestors. This 1,000-year-old legacy also survives in the Norman patois and in the names of towns and villages: old Norman words like *beuf* (shelter), *bec* (stream) and *tot* (piece of land) are still spoken today in place-names such as Elbeuf, Bolbec, Yvetot. Another reflection of the Viking heritage is the Norman seafaring tradition. Long before the great Portuguese and Spanish voyages of discovery, sailors from Dieppe, Le Havre and Honfleur were sailing to Newfoundland, Africa, Brazil, Sumatra and Canada. Champlain, the founder of Quebec, was a Norman sea-captain. The presence of this tradition can perhaps be felt even more strongly in the little fishing villages of the Pays de Caux than in big ports like Le Havre, Cherbourg and Rouen.

The Seine plays a scarcely less important role than the sea in Norman life. This great waterway leading to the heart of Paris has played a key strategic and economic role in the history of Normandy for over 1,000 years. The majestic, undulating green landscape of the Seine valley, from the Vexin chalk plateau to the Pays de Caux and Le Havre, seems a haven of peace and tranquillity. But it is no stranger to the horrors of war. The traveller who follows the Seine

Rouen: Rue Martainville.

downstream from Paris will know that he is leaving the Ile de France and entering Normandy when he sees the massive ruined fortress of **Château-Gaillard**. This fantastic piece of medieval architecture, with its towers, keeps, ramparts, galleries and labyrinthine tunnels, was built in the 12th century by Richard the Lionheart to bar the way between Paris and Rouen. It was a vain undertaking, for in 1204 the fortress was captured by the French King Philip Augustus, after a siege lasting five months. Later, Henri IV ordered Château-Gaillard to be razed to the ground, but today, on its rugged hilltop overlooking the town of Les Andelys, its ruins still make an impressive sight.

A little further downstream, silhouetted against the soft light of the Norman sky, rise the church towers of Rouen, the intellectual and economic capital of eastern Normandy. The old quarters of Rouen, which miraculously survived the bombing in World War II, contain **ancient timber-framed houses**, the old market-place where Joan of Arc was burned at the stake on 30 May 1431, fine churches such as those of St. Maclou and St. Ouen (its 82-metre-high tower surmounted with a crown), and the cathedral of Notre-Dame, of which Monet made many studies. In old **Rouen** time seems to stand still and the atmosphere of the Middle Ages lingers on. The port, however, hums with activity, as long lines of barges wait to be loaded from cargo boats from all over the world.

Caen: the Abbaye aux Hommes.

The manor of Coupesarte, Calvados.

uriant Pays d'Auge and the famous seaside resorts of Deauville, Trouville and Cabourg.

Even today Caen abounds with memories of that distant time when France and England nearly became one. William the Conqueror and his Queen, Matilda, lived in the castle, which today houses a fine museum. William and Matilda also built **the abbaye aux Hommes** (today the church of St. Etienne) where the Conqueror is buried, and the abbaye aux Dames (today the church of the Trinity), Matilda's resting place. These fine buildings gave birth to a highly characteristic Norman romanesque style, austere and pure. In nearby Bayeux, the world's most sumptuous and elaborate comic strip, Queen Matilda's tapestry, tells the story of the Norman conquest of England in 58 meticulously embroidered scenes.

Around Caen lies a welcoming district of lush green meadows, crystal-blue rivers, thick hedges and rounded apple-trees. During the Renaissance period, manor-houses of wood and varnished brick replaced the fortified châteaux in Normandy. Perhaps one of the most charming of these is **the manor of Coupesarte**, near Livarot, whose gleaming timberwork and delicate towers cast their reflection over sleepy waters.

The same peaceful atmosphere reigns as far as the sea, and along the stretches of coastline known as the "Côte de Grâce" and the "Côte Fleurie". On the former, which stretches from the Seine estuary to that of the Touques, is the picturesque town of **Honfleur**. This once-prosperous port was long ago dethroned by Le Havre, on the opposite bank of the Seine estuary, but it still casts its unique magic spell, with its calm inner harbour, its seamen's houses as tall and narrow as old ships, and the picturesque wooden church of St. Catherine, built in the 15th century by Honfleur's carpenters.

Along the right bank of the Seine, the road climbs from the abbey of St. Wandrille to that of Jumièges, which in the 7th century was one of the main centres of Western mysticism. Today all that remains of them are brooding ruins gazing out over magnificent countryside—the outline of the original buildings, their massive walls and perfectly shaped vaulting.

Downstream from Rouen lies Caudebec. Here, at the time of the great equinoctial tides, crowds of visitors flock to see an immense tidal wave surge up the Seine. Further downstream still are Tancarville, where Europe's biggest suspension bridge,

1,420 metres long, spans the waters of the estuary, and Le Havre. Today France's second biggest commercial port, Le Havre was for more than a century the port of embarkation of great trans-Atlantic liners.

Le Havre is the hub of eastern Normandy and the lower Seine valley. Its counterpart in central Normandy is the major port of Caen, once known as the "Athens of Normandy" because of the dynamism of its intellectual life. It dominates the region at the very heart of Normandy—Normandy at its richest, and, one might say, most Norman—the valley of the river Bessin, the lux-

West of the Côte de Grâce lies a stretch of coast known as the Côte Fleurie (the "coast of flowers") which has attracted holidaymakers for over a century. Trouville was a favourite resort of Flaubert and Dumas, while its neighbour, Deauville, was promoted by the Duc de Morny during the Second Empire. Since then many international figures, as well as all the leading personalities in the French arts, literature, show business and finance, have strolled at some time or other along Deauville's famous "planches", the boardwalks which stretch along the edge of the beach. Further along the coast, in the same landscape of wooded hills, grassy plains, beaches and sanddunes, are a number of smaller towns such as Lion, Luc-sur-Mer, Colleville, Saint-Laurent and Vierville, which were once simply known as quiet family resorts. Today these places are associated with a roll-call of grimmer names—Juno Beach, Gold Beach, Omaha Beach—for on June 6, 1944 this quiet area stepped dramatically into history as the scene of the allied landings.

West along the coast from the little town of Port-en-Bessin begins the Cotentin peninsula whose beaches also have sinister memories of the 1944 landings. Some of the wounds inflicted on the Cotentin then took long to heal. All that remained of Saint-Lô was its cathedral. At Valognes (a historic town which has its place in French literary history through the work of the 19th-century writer Barbey d'Aurevilly) only one of the opulent 17th- and 18th-century town houses is still standing. Coutances, from which the Cotentin takes its name, was also flattened by bombing, but its fine Gothic cathedral miraculously survived, with its soaring twin spires which seem to defy the laws of gravity.

But the Cotentin has many other attractions for the visitor: its rugged, secretive scenery, its windswept coastline, its granite houses and the gloomy legends associated with its moorland. South of the peninsula begins the *bocage*, whose lofty hills, thick woods and swift-flowing streams, stretching eastwards from the granite peaks of Brittany, have earned it the name of "Suisse Normande" (Norman Switzerland). And on the shores of the Atlantic, where Normandy and Brittany meet, rises the spire of **Mont-Saint-Michel**.

Whether Mont-Saint-Michel is Breton or Norman is a long-disputed question. Whatever the answer, it is undeniable that the rock is a place where men have gathered to worship ever since the dawn of time. When **the Norman "Charitons"**, members of a fraternity founded in the Middle Ages to ensure that the dead were given a Christian burial, walk in procession at Mont-Saint-Michel, wearing their embroidered costumes and carrying their banners and their bells, they tread in the footsteps of the old pilgrims to Compostella, who broke their journey there.

Mont Saint-Michel.
The pilgrimage of the "Charitons" to Mont Saint-Michel.

A Norman horse-dealer.

The rock was converted to Christianity by St. Auber, bishop of Avranches, acting on the orders—so tradition has it—of St. Michael the Archangel. But profoundly Christian that it is, this jewel of western architecture retains its links with an earlier magical tradition.

In summer its mystical beauty is spoiled by the teeming crowds and the souvenir shops. But in winter Mont-Saint-Michel comes back into its own when solitude descends, the cold winds blow and the waves hammer against the walls. This is an ideal time to walk along the ramparts, wander up and down the stone steps, see the old house where the great 14th-century soldier Du Guesclin lived, visit the abbey and admire the buildings on three storeys, dating from the 11th to the 15th-century, which are known as the "merveille" and include the almonry, the knights' room and the cloister with its 240 red granite pillars. Winter is also the time to remember the Benedictine monks who built the abbey and named it "St. Michel in peril of the sea".

The perils of the sea are also much in evidence a little further along the coast at Granville, once a pirate stronghold known as the "Monaco of the north", perched on a granite rock 80 metres above the sea. Its ramparts have survived from the days of the great pirate expeditions. The upper town dates from the 18th-century. In 1793 Granville was the scene of a bloody episode of the French Revolution. The "chouans", royalist counter-revolutionaries, were waiting for the arrival of the English fleet to help them capture the town. They were repelled and massacred, and the great 19th-century historian Michelet later wrote of the "strong, fresh, healthy wind" from Granville. During the Second Empire, Stendhal and Victor Hugo made Granville better known to the outside world. From Granville boats leave for Jersey and the 300 granite islands and islets of Chausey.

This, then, is Normandy. Almost Breton in the west, almost Picard in the east, it does have a profound unity of its own. Ever since the foundation of the duchy of Normandy, this land of earthy individualists and adventurous sailors, with its mercantile dynamism and tradition of mysticism, has always presented an image of harmony. It is a meeting-point of civilizations, from each of which it has absorbed and reshaped those elements which suited it best. Even today Normandy still keeps its sense of proportion and a disposition for acting only after careful reflection. It welcomes tourists without allowing them to submerge its identity, and encourages industry without sacrificing its traditional activities.

Some of France's greatest writers have been Normans—among them Malherbe, Corneille and Flaubert, while painters since the precursors of Impressionism have been drawn to Normandy to try to capture the fleeting movements of its light. But Normandy is also—and this is not the least of its charms—a place where people take unconcealed pleasure in the delights of the table.

Today the Normans rarely wear their **traditional costume** of blue smock, checked scarf and jaunty cap, except on special occasions. But **the**

apple-trees still blossom in the meadows, the air is as soft as ever, the pleasure-boats still unfurl their sails in peaceful harbours, and Normandy still lives up to its reputation as a welcoming and rewarding place to visit.

Apple-blossom time in Normandy.

2

Picardy and Artois

A sky of billowing clouds; ploughed fields rippling as far as the eye can see; rich, heavy soil broken up by gently-flowing streams and shimmering canals. Such are the dominant features of the great plain of Picardy and Artois, which stretches from the gates of Paris to the North Sea in one direction and to the mountains of Asia in the other. Lacking natural defences, it has been invaded time and time again, witnessing some of Europe's bloodiest fighting from the Middle Ages until recent times. This region seems fated to be simply a thoroughfare, a pawn sometimes of strategic, sometimes of economic importance. Millions have passed through it; few can claim to know it well. Today the hub of the Common Market, it deserves to be better known, for it has much to offer: opulent, majestic scenery; a wealth of archaeological remains and a rich architectural heritage; the still-unspoilt beauty of the Bay of the Somme; and long, sandy beaches swept by bracing sea winds.

With its 400,000 hectares of arable land, 83,000 hectares of meadows, and 50,000 hectares of forest, the region at first gives the impression of some gigantic field stretching uninterrupted from the Paris region to Artois—a vast expanse of wheat and the beet crops grown either for animal feed or for sugar. The people of Picardy today farm the land intensively, using the latest agricultural machinery and industrial farming techniques. They are the heirs to a tradition stretching back to the Middle Ages, whereby every square metre of land is used to the full, an attitude noted in 1701 by a royal official, who recorded that Picardy had less uncultivated land than any other French province. But while intensive farming is practised in the big upland villages hemmed in by protective clumps of fruit-trees, market gardening is a major activity in the valleys, on low-lying marshy ground which once provided rough hunting and fishing. Around Amiens, for example, flat-bottomed boats with raised prows (known as "bateaux à cornet") ply through a strange poetic landscape of water gardens. Vegetables, flowers, herbs and fruit-trees grow on rectangular islands surrounded by canals. These market gardens, known as the **"hortillonnages" of the Somme** are unique. In the past their produce was sold only in the nearby towns, but today they play an important role in the economy of the whole region. A small-scale canning and preserving industry has been developed for this produce, which is now marketed as far away as the Paris region.

Hortillonnages of the Somme near Amiens.

The Opal Coast.

Small-scale industry developed in many scattered villages of Picardy at a comparatively early date, often transforming the tenor of village life. But while this industrial development halted the widespread emigration of countrymen who had been drawn to Paris in search of work (during the 17th century, for example, in the time of Molière, valets often bore the name of Picard) it did not alter the essentially rural character of Picardy.

In this region, where the land takes pride of place in people's lives, the coast is a world entirely apart. Some of the ports of Picardy, such as Abbeville, enjoyed great prosperity in the Middle Ages, when their importance was second only to that of Dieppe and Caen. But as the Somme estuary gradually silted up and nearby Le Havre rose to prominence, they fell by the wayside. The coastal towns of Picardy's **Opal Coast** now live mainly off the tourist trade. The climate is cool but bracing, and so rich in ozone that French doctors often recommend a stay here as a rest-cure for both children and adults. At Berck-Plage, where France's Child Welfare Board established its first children's hospital in 1864, the air is so pure that it only contains 4 bacteria to the cubic metre, against an average of 900,000 in Paris. Immense beaches of fine sand, high sand dunes and pine trees provide the perfect setting for a children's holiday. Before World War II Le Touquet, with its unmistakably English atmosphere, was one of France's most elegant resorts, and is still an important centre for tennis, golf and horse-riding. Linked to England by regular air services, Le Touquet must surely contain more English visitors to the square metre than anywhere else in France: more than a quarter of its visitors come from across the Channel. Along the coast from the Authie river to the Somme, summer resorts lie scattered among the pine trees. Visitors can fish and shoot among the sand dunes at Fort-Mahon and Quend-Plage. Le Crotoy and Saint-Valery are ideal bases for exploring the Somme estuary, whose harsh landscape seems to have survived unchanged since the dawn of time. Thousands of migrating birds break their journeys in the bay of the Somme, and an unending (and eventful) battle goes on between hunters and conservationists, who have recently succeeded in setting up a wild fowl reserve at Saint-Quentin-en-Tourmont.

Further north along the pine-fringed sandy coast, between the river Canche and the Cap d'Alprech are the resorts of Sainte-Cécile, Equihen-Plage and Hardelot, where the Boulonnais cliffs begin. They attract many week-end visitors, mainly from the surrounding area, but as yet they are not invaded by hordes of summer visitors. From the limestone headland of Cap d'Alprech the coastline curves northwards to Cap Gris Nez and then northeast to Cap Blanc Nez. Nestling among the greenery are a number of small seaside resorts where families scramble over the rocks looking for crabs and mussels. Close by Cap d'Alprech is the beautiful and as yet unspoilt little fishing village of Le Portel. A little further north is **Boulogne-sur-Mer**, France's most important fishing port. Although the town was severely damaged in the war, the 18th-century château in the upper town has survived. A few kilometres away is the site of the camp where Napoleon's troops assembled for the planned invasion of England in 1804. A column standing in the middle of parkland commemorates the spot. However, this piece of history is less important than the cross-Channel ferries in bringing the tourists to Boulogne. Each year a million people and 150,000 cars pass through the town, the main port of entry for British visitors to France. Along the

coast to the north, the 50-metre-high headland of Cap Gris Nez looks out over the busy Straits of Dover. From its foot a fine sandy beach stretches for 13 kilometres to the even higher cliffs of Cap Blanc Nez, 134 metres above sea level. Between these two headlands lies Wissant, thought to be the site of Portus Itius, from where Julius Caesar sailed to conquer Britain.

Its geographical position between Flanders and England and its semi-agricultural, semi-industrial way of life have made Picardy one of the most densely populated parts of France. There is a village or small town at every cross-roads and every railway or canal junction. Important towns such as Abbeville, La Fère, and above all Amiens, also grew up around the bridges which spanned Picardy's broad rivers. Amiens, the capital of western Picardy, was badly damaged in World War II. Rebuilt by the French architect Auguste Perret, it today has a modern 30-storey tower, taller than the spire of its great cathedral, though less spiritually inspiring.

Gothic architecture was born in Picardy, perhaps at Morienval near Crépy-en-Valois, where an unpretentious and somewhat heavy example of the style can be seen in the ambulatory of the abbey church of Notre-Dame.

Boulogne, the fish docks.

Amiens cathedral: the great rose window.

Reacting against the Romanesque style, whose austere purity it sought to replace with a soaring aspiration towards the divine, Gothic architecture took firm root in Picardy after this modest beginning. With its six cathedrals, the province has an outstanding place in the history of medieval architecture. (Picardy's modern Départements—the Aisne, the Oise and the Somme—thus have more cathedrals than any other three Départements in France.) **Amiens cathedral** is the biggest in France and possibly the most moving. Its stones, its carvings, its stained glass (sadly damaged by war) and its beautiful **great rose window** express the mystery of faith with indescribable profundity. The stalls are carved with thousands of figures from the Bible and everyday life. The figure of Christ between the central doors of the main portal, known as the Beau Dieu d'Amiens, displays all the feeling and inner force of a religion which, while searching for intellectual depth, nevertheless seeks to maintain contact with its congregation of believers. On the base of the west front the labours of the twelve months of the year are depicted, along with the signs of the zodiac. The meticulous and spirited craftsmanship of this calendar, which shows many aspects of life in 13th-century Picardy, has won it a well-deserved reputation as one of the great masterpieces of medieval art.

Not far from Amiens, in the Thiérache district between the Oise and Sambre rivers, one can still see the fortified churches of Beaurain, Marly, Englancourt, Saint Algis and Wimy, where peasants once took refuge as marauding soldiers swept through. At Coucy-le-Château the imposing ruins of the fortress still stand and at Péronne are the remains of a castle with four round towers. Houses dating from the fourth millenium B.C. have been discovered at Cuiry-les-Chaudardes, the oldest village in France, and it was at Abbeville in the 19th century that the French scholar Boucher de Perthes unearthed some flint instruments in the sands of the Somme, a key event in the development of palaeontology.

Amiens cathedral: the nave.

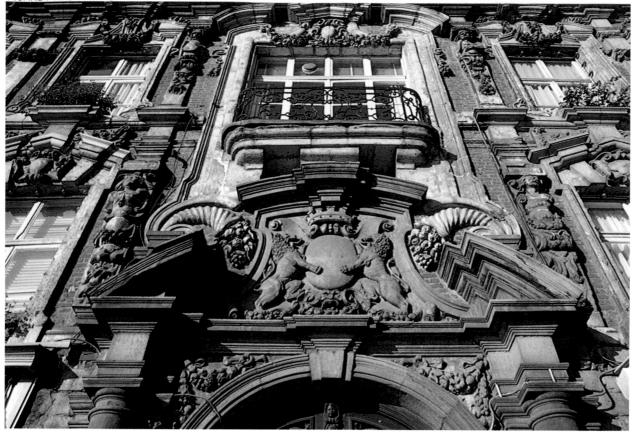

Lille, the old Bourse.

The *gayants* of Douai.

Canal scene in northern France.

Arras, the Grande Place.

Saint-Quentin is the major centre of eastern Picardy, the counterpart to Amiens in the west. It dominates a region devoted to farming and the textile industry.

Beyond Saint-Quentin begin the gentle hills of the Cambrésis, and beyond Amiens the hills of Artois. Beneath them, on a vast plain stretching from the Ardennes forest to Cap Gris Nez, is France's "Black Country", the industrial region which plays a vital role in the country's economic life. People who do not know the area often imagine it to be a grim, desolate place, and it is true that parts of it have been polluted and scarred by industrial development. Nevertheless, the plain is more than just a sprawl of coal-mines, pit villages and patches of waste ground. Its attractive features include the rolling green valley of the Sambre river, also known as the "Normandy of the north", and the forest of Raismes whose tall trees stretch as far as the spa town of Saint-Amand-les-Eaux, which specializes in the treatment of rheumatism. **The calm waters of the canals** reflect an often turbulent sky, a juxtaposition of opposites which in a sense sums up the people of northern France. They are both realists and dreamers, hard and kindly, ostentatious and modest, suspicious yet—once the ice is broken—hospitable. For the student of history this is an area of matchless interest. In the huge Lille-Roubaix-Turcoing urban complex (of which Dunkirk now forms part) the factories which light up the night skies make a striking contrast with fine old town houses.

Strong reminders that Artois once belonged to Spain can still be seen in its architecture, its customs and sometimes in the physical appearance of its people. **The gayants of Douai** provide one direct link with the period of the Spanish occupation. Huge figures representing fierce popular heroes of that time, they are paraded through the streets in great pomp. So often and so bitterly disputed by Burgundians, Spaniards and the French, won at such cost by Louis XIV, so often threatened and invaded, ravaged and rebuilt, Artois today takes great pride in its ancient traditions.

Lille, Douai and Arras owe their prosperity to the textile industry, which has made them important bargaining counters in European history from the Middle Ages until modern times. A well-to-do middle class, not unafraid to flaunt its wealth a little, has left its imprint on the architecture of each of these old towns. **The Old Bourse of Lille**, built in the middle of the 17th century, is a typical example of a style which is heavily ornate but always calm and harmonious. Somewhat more austere are the fine gabled houses in **the Grande Place** and the Petite Place of **Arras**, the capital of Artois, which was largely rebuilt in 1919. These two linked and arcaded squares are a fine example of French Flemish architecture.

The Meuse at Monthermé.

3

Lorraine and Champagne

As the morning mists drift skywards from the river, one can still imagine the four pious knights of legend—the four sons of Aymon—galloping down the majestic **valley of the Meuse** towards the town of Monthermé. The western slopes of the blue-tinged Vosges highlands, pitted with glistening lakes, rise in the distance, before tumbling steeply down to Alsace on their eastern side. Today passes such as the **Col de la Schlucht** penetrate the sombre forests of firs and cross this mountain barrier. Between the Vosges massif and that of the Ardennes, each worn down by the long erosion of time and weather, lies a region of hills and a long, fertile plain. This countryside of welcoming villages and orchards, with its heady, full-bodied golden wines made from grapes ripened in the Moselle sun, is Lorraine.

Crossed by the main traffic routes linking the Benelux countries and Germany with the Mediterranean, Lorraine, apparently so open to the outside world, is in fact a region of stubborn particularism. The traveller who approaches Lorraine from Paris must first cross Champagne, with its wealth of medieval masterpieces. Clovis was baptised and many French kings were crowned in Rheims cathedral, one of the finest gems of Gothic architecture. The

The Col de la Schlucht.

abbey church of Saint-Rémi, also in Rheims, has been described as a "meeting-point of Carolingian and Romanesque art". In Troyes, the ancient capital of Champagne, timber-framed dwellings in narrow streets stand as reminders of a distant past. And of course Champagne boasts France's most famous vineyards. But this sparkling reputation should not obscure the fact that Champagne has been the scene of brutal wars and battles such as those of Valmy, Sedan and the Marne, which changed the course of French history.

The Meuse at Domrémy.

Nancy: the Place Stanislas.

East of Champagne lies that part of the ancient medieval kingdom of Lotharingia which became the duchy of Lorraine. Ever since it was established between the 10th and 13th centuries, Lorraine has always been so profoundly French, despite wars, shifting frontiers, all the processes of historical change, that its emblem, the double-barred cross of Lorraine, is today the national emblem of France. This curious region, only 350 kilometres from Paris, is in many ways an outpost of eastern Europe. Its climate of icy winters and scorching summers is Central European, like its changing scenery, now dark and mysterious, now soft and gentle as a Polish lullaby. Even its rivers steer clear of the west: they avoid the Seine, the Channel and even the nearby Paris basin. They all flow into the North Sea, after joining the Moselle, the Meuse and the Rhine. And yet for all that, there is a whiff of the Mediterranean in the air of Lorraine: the villages nestling between hill and plain are roofed with tiles that are almost Provençal. And instead of sloping steeply, as in most parts of eastern France, these roofs are practically flat. Even the French-based patois spoken over most of the area (Germanic dialects are less common in Lorraine than French) sometimes lilts with the melodic rhythms of the South of France.

Lorraine's most famous figure is the humble shepherdess known to history as Joan of Arc. **The Meuse**, so often crimson with the blood of men, flows through her native village of **Domrémy.** The cottage where she was born still stands. One day when she was watching over her sheep in the nearby forest known as the Bois-Chenu, sitting beneath an ancient tree, she heard voices ordering her to drive the English out of France. Today a basilica marks this spot where the course of French history was changed. But despite Joan of Arc's fame, Domrémy was to remain a humble village, overshadowed then as now by the nearby city of **Nancy**, capital of Lorraine. Medieval and classical quarters stand side by side in Nancy, but its greatest architectural glory, **the Place Stanislas**, is a masterpiece of pure classical style. It was built by a Polish king, Stanislas Leczinski. The story goes that Louis XV "presented" Stanislas, his father-in-law, with the duchy of Lorraine, which had recently come into his hands from François III, duke of Lorraine. Europe was then discovering the art of grandiose town planning, and to please their new sovereign an architect, Emmanuel Héré, and an ironsmith, Jean Lamour, enclosed the former Place Royal with wrought-iron railings ornamented with gold leaf. Inside the square they laid out pavilions and a walk known as La Pépinière, and between a triumphal arch and the Hôtel de Ville created a magnificent setting for royal festivities and celebrations, studded with fountains and ornamental pools.

Metz: the cathedral of Saint-Etienne.

Metz: La Porte des Allemands (The Gateway of the Germans).

History has treated Lorraine harshly, for Europe's wars have rarely spared her. At Verdun, on the Meuse, are many reminders of the terrible eight months during World War I when Frenchmen and Germans were locked in combat in blood-drenched mud. Every spot in the surrounding countryside bears a name associated with acts of heroism which have become legendary—names like the Fort de Vaux, the Bois des Caures, the Mort-Homme, are now inscribed in French history, along with that of Douaumont, the most famous of all, site of a great memorial to the battle. These lovely valleys and fertile fields have probably seen more violent deaths than anywhere else in the world. Men have fought here since the dawn of time. This gentle land so charged with drama has always been the most sensitive point in France's armour. It was at Verdun as early as 843 that the treaty dividing up Charlemagne's empire was signed, sowing the seeds of countless future disputes. Before the 20th century, the most famous of these involved the 16th-century French king Henri II and the Emperor Charles V in a contest over Metz, Toul and Verdun. The Emperor laid siege to Metz, which put up a heroic and successful resistance.

Rising above the river, **the cathedral of Saint-Étienne, in Metz**, is worthy of comparison with those of Beauvais and Amiens. It is as lofty as they are, and has the same power and harmonious proportions. Its windows are vast, and its stained glass is beautiful.

Another landmark in Metz is the 13th-century **Porte des Allemands** (Gateway of the Germans) built by the Teutonic knights, who also founded a hospital in the city. One can imagine from looking at the esplanade, the Place d'Armes and the Porte Serpenoise, that old Metz must have been a magnificently-designed citadel-town. An important settlement ever since Gallo-Roman times (Gallo-Roman traces still survive in various parts of the city), Metz is the traditional rival of Nancy.

Between the coal-mining basin on the Saar border and the iron deposits to the north of the Moselle (especially along the Orne river) are beautiful forests and undulating agricultural land. The roads are bordered with fruit-trees: mirabelle and quetsch plums, pear- and apple-trees. But the wealth of Lorraine lies chiefly underground: its iron deposits are the third richest in the world. Besides Metz and Nancy, three other towns of Lorraine call for mention. Toul, which stands on a bend in the Moselle, is an ancient bishopric and garrison town, whose ramparts were built by Vauban. Baccarat, on the edge of the Vosges, has been famed for its crystal-ware since the Middle Ages. And at Lunéville, on the Meurthe river, the 18th-century duke Leopold of Lorraine, dazzled by the splendour of Louis XIV's palace, built a château designed to emulate Versailles.

The Lake of Longemer in the Vosges.

Industry is far from all-pervasive in Lorraine, although it is vital to the balance of the region's economy and a prolonged shortage of jobs would drain away its life-blood. No sooner has one left behind the industrial towns of Rombas, Hayange, or Thionville, Lorraine's major steel-making centre, than one finds oneself deep in the countryside, surrounded by ploughed fields and grazing herds. Orchards and vineyards grow on the Woëvre plain and along the "Côte"—the steep wooded escarpment dominating hill-slopes where straggling villages huddle. Once, Lorraine was covered with vineyards, but today all that remains are those on the hills rising from the Meuse and Moselle valleys, the "Côtes de Meuse" and the

The Vosges forest.

"Côtes de Moselle", the lone survivors of a phylloxera epidemic which struck at the beginning of this century. Lovingly cared for and nursed back to life, these vineyards today produce abundant quantities of delicious "grey wine", just the thing to drink before climbing beneath the firs and spruces towards the deep, dark lakes around Gérardmer and then on to the ridge of the Vosges. These still lakes have magical, evocative names— **the Lac de Longemer,** the Lac de Blanchemer, the Lac de Retournemer. Some lines by Paul Verlaine, one of Lorraine's most famous sons, spring to mind as one leaves this region in the direction of the sombre, little-known yet beautiful Ardennes:

There are woods without number in the land of my father.
There the eyes of wolves sometimes glisten in the night.
And black is the myrtle at the foot of the green oak tree.

33

Alsace

Alsace became part of France in 1648 by the Treaty of Westphalia, which ended the Thirty Years War. When Louis XIV first looked out over his new province from the hill-slopes of the Vosges a few years later, he is supposed to have exclaimed in admiration: "Quel beau jardin!"

Alsace today is industrialized and has seen many other changes since the 17th century, but, protected by its two great natural boundaries, the Vosges and the Rhine, it is still essentially the "beautiful garden" which enchanted Louis XIV. Vine-covered hills still slope gently down from the rocky crests of the Vosges to the Alsatian plain; the plain itself is still a lovely patchwork of meadows, woods, wheatfields and orchards, furrowed by rivers renowned for their fishing; the mighty Rhine still waters the "garden" in the east. If it was ever decided to grant special "protected" status to those regions of France which have succeeded in preserving their character, their landscape, their traditions and their architectural heritage, Alsace would be one of the best-qualified candidates.

Alsace consists of three distinct areas—a plain, wooded hillsides and high mountains—which are totally interdependent. Without the two others none of them could function economically or socially as it does today. Since ancient times Alsace has been the meeting-place and melting-pot of two different civilizations: a Latin, wine-drinking civilization and a Germanic, beer-drinking civilization. They have lived together in a constant process of interaction, creating a unique cultural setting. The heart and symbol of this cultural intermixture is the city of **Strasbourg**, with its **steeply sloping rooftops** and its great **cathedral** whose pink sandstone spire soars 140 metres into the sky.

The cathedral and old roofs of Strasbourg.

Strasbourg: Petite France.

the march of time. When midday strikes, the apostles pass before Christ, who blesses them, while a cock beats its wings three times in memory of St. Peter's denial of Christ.

Beneath the cathedral lies the city, yesterday a regional capital and today, as the seat of the Council of Europe, a contender for the title of capital of Europe. Beyond the Orangerie park are Strasbourg's modern quarters, its university and the Maison de l'Europe, headquarters of the Council of Europe. Strasbourg owes much of its prosperity to the Rhine. Its port is the fifth most important in France, and the river now links Alsace with northern Europe and the North Sea, while the Rhône-Rhine canal will soon link the region with the Mediterranean as well. But far more important than the mighty Rhine as a factor in Strasbourg's charm is its tributary, the Ill, spanned by covered bridges. It meanders through the old quarter known as **Petite France**, where old houses gaze down on their shifting reflections in this tranquil river. Fronting the narrow twisting streets are many fine old timber-framed dwellings, whose silhouettes are reminiscent of children's cardboard castles, each storey being progressively narrower than the one beneath it. Many peaceful and charming dwellings await discovery, the homes of the rich fishermen, tanners, brewers and boatmen who brought wealth to Strasbourg. It is pleasant to stroll from the Place du Marché aux Poissons (where boats leave for a tour of the city) as far as the Quai des Bateliers and the Pont du Corbeau, where the Hostellerie du Corbeau still stands virtually unchanged since the 16th century, when it was a celebrated inn. The charming **Musée Alsacien** nearby has a fine collection of everyday objects ranging from the humble to the magnificent.

Strasbourg cathedral, with its tremendous single spire rising above the city streets, was for centuries one of the world's tallest buildings. The meticulous craftsmen who created this serene masterpiece of Gothic architecture used the lovely pink sandstone of the Vosges to create a matchless interpretation of man's yearning for the divine, such as the perfectly-proportioned façade and the sublime thirteenth-century Angels' pillar in the south transept. But although its beauty is timeless, Strasbourg cathedral possesses a remarkable reminder of time's relentlessness, in the form of its famous astronomical clock. The planets (whose movements have been calculated into an infinite future), the apostles and Christ himself all record

Strasbourg:
exhibition of
regional desserts
at the Musée
Alsacien.

In rural Alsace today life goes on much as it did in the past. Many village houses are furnished with gleaming old cupboards, wardrobes and dressers and are heated with superb faience stoves. Each year the wine-growers proudly wear their traditional costumes at the wine-harvest celebrations. Traditional moulds are brought out once a year for making the family's Christmas sweet-meats. Each house has its parlour, its "Sunday room", where all the family's most treasured possessions are kept. Lovingly cleaned, it is only used on high days and holidays. Many houses still have old wooden shutters.

The Kammerzell house situated on the Place de la Cathédrale is a lovely early Renaissance structure; its façade is covered with ornate carvings. A fine selection of medieval sculpture and painting can be seen in the city's Œuvre Notre-Dame museum, itself dating from the Middle Ages. Another fine Strasbourg building is the eighteenth-century Palais des Rohan, once an episcopal palace, whose terrace overlooks the Ill river.

Strasbourg has a long tradition as a centre of freedom and toleration. From the Middle Ages until the Thirty Years War, it headed a group of ten free cities known as the "Decapole", which achieved and upheld the virtual autonomy of this part of Europe. It was in Strasbourg that Gutenberg set up the first printing press. Protestants were allowed complete freedom of worship. And it was in the house of the first mayor of Strasbourg, Dietrich, that Rouget de Lisle first sang his "song of the men of Marseilles", later to become the French national anthem. From Strasbourg to Colmar a road winds southwards across the plain. This is the famous "route des vins", which leads through vineyards where in late summer the grapes ripen in golden sunlight. Alsatian wines owe their sweetness and their full-bodied flavour to the hot, dry summers, the vineyards being protected from the rain-bearing winds by the Vosges mountains in the west. Among the vineyards and plum and cherry orchards, the road runs through large villages, many of them set in protective folds of the hills and built around a paved square.

One of the most charming and characteristic of these townships which live from farming and wine-growing is **Riquewihr**, one of the few to have given its name to an Alsatian wine. In Riquewihr, as in all these old towns, life seems to focus on the fountain in the square, where children meet and play and the old sit and gossip. The old wooden houses with their gables, carved beams and loggias still bear the names of the men who built them hundreds of years ago: the Liebrich house, dating from the 16th century; the Preis-Zimmer house, once an inn; the 17th-century Jung house; the stone-built Dissler house and the Kiener house with its bas-relicf depiction of Death seizing the man who built it.

Strasbourg: the Kammerzell house.

Riquewihr.

The château of Haut-Kœnigsbourg.

Along the "route des vins" lie many other villages, such as Wangen, Molsheim, Rosheim and Obernai, whose names call to mind the Riesling and Traminer wines they produce. It was near to Obernai that Sainte Odile, the patron saint of Alsace, founded a convent long ago in the 7th century, surrounded by nine castles which are today no more than ruins. Perched on a gentle hilltop, **Zellenberg** seems to rise from a sea of vines.

But the vineyards and orchards of Alsace contain other, grimmer memories of the past: the "wine road" has often echoed to the tramp of marching feet. There are few reminders of World War II—except for crosses in the cemeteries. But earlier wars left more permanent traces in the form of mighty fortresses perched on virtually inaccessible peaks, their towers, battlements and thick stone walls dominating the plain, forest and river below. Brooding and romantic, these Alsatian *burgs* evoke a sense of power and drama, unlike the fortresses of the Auvergne and Languedoc which in some ways they resemble. Some of the most notable of these eyries are the château of Kintzheim which today houses a collection of birds of prey; the château of Saint-Ulrich near Ribeauvillé; and, most impressive of all, **Haut-Kœnigsbourg**, between Sélestat and Ribeauvillé, a castle with which many dark legends are associated. Approached by a dizzily-curving road, the massive walls of Haut-Kœnigsbourg seem the perfect setting for some bloody historical tragedy.

Zellenberg.

Kaysersberg.

Riquewihr.

Ribeauvillé: wood-block printing on cloth.

An Alsatian bride.

In the streets of Barr.

The manufacture of Munster cheese.

Today these forbidding fortresses survive only as grim reminders of a martial past to an age when European wars seem thankfully to be over for good. They feed the imagination of fantasy-lovers, but that is all. The old battle-scars have healed. In the villages of Alsace, on the other hand, the people still cling to traditions of a more peaceful kind. **Kaysersberg**, **Riquewihr** and **Barr** seem scarcely to have changed for centuries. Walking through one of these villages, with their dominant tones of ochre, faded pink and off-white, is like walking through the stage-set for a historical play. The houses jut forward into the street, with their half-timbered facades, carved corner-posts, fretted shutters and elaborately decorated doors. Almost all of them have carved double doors, lovingly cleaned and polished, still evoking the trees from which they were hewn. The tradition of carpentry is still strong in Alsace, and these doors, no two of which are identical, are still made today almost exactly as they were in the past.

Some Alsatian towns and villages specialize in a single trade or craft. **Ribeauvillé**, for example, is one of the few places in France where **wood-block printing on cloth** is still done, using techniques handed down from generation to generation. The fine blue and white checked cloth called "kœlsh" is also still woven in Ribeauvillé's workshops.

Another ancient tradition is still carried on in the high pastureland (known as the "Chaumes") which lies above the forests of the Vosges. This is **the manufacture of Munster cheese**, which was introduced into the area in the 7th century, by the monks of the earliest abbeys to be founded in Alsace, who in a sense colonized the region and brought civilization to it. According to tradition, the herds climb up to the Chaumes from the valleys at the end of May, and graze there until September under the watchful eye of the *marcaire*, the herdsman who is also cheese-maker. The cheese, known as Munster cheese after the abbey of Munster, was made during this season before being sold and exported in wooden boxes which were also made on the spot. In the past, the people of the valleys badly needed the extra money they could earn from making and selling cheese, but with the coming of industry to Alsace and the consequent increase in job-opportunities, less and less cheese was made. The farmhouses on the high pastures were gradually abandoned or else converted into tourist hotels. Today, however, there is a resurgence of interest in this type of farming and cheese-making.

Old traditions thus still live on in all the towns and villages of Alsace. When the Alsatians put on their beautiful old costumes for the "Johannisfeuer" (the feast of St. John) or the "Kelva" (traditional festival held in the mountain villages) they do not always do it at the request of the local tourist board.

Further south along the "route des vins" lies Colmar, still the major tourist centre of Alsace, although its role as economic and political capital of the region now belongs to Strasbourg. **Beneath a mantle of snow, Colmar** looks like an illustration for one of the folk-tales which abound in Alsace, and for many people this lovely old town sums up the Alsatian character: warm-heartedness and gaiety concealed beneath a rugged exterior. With its pretty gabled houses overlooking calm waterways, it brings to mind Bruges and Amsterdam, but its attraction is unique. Flat-bottomed boats glide slowly along the channels, pushing aside floating grasses, past gardens, moss-covered wash-houses and ancient walls festooned with climbing plants. The lines of the buildings slant crookedly, as unplanned and untidy as life itself. The streets twist and turn haphazardly until suddenly, unexpectedly, one emerges into a curious, asymmetrical square. In this town which tugs at the heart-strings, even the most beautiful buildings have an air of effortless simplicity. The housefronts with their jutting beams or loggias, in many cases carved with baroque motifs, date from Colmar's most glorious period when it owed its prosperity exclusively to wine. Almost all the dwellings which have survived from this period, such as the Pfister house, are still known by their original names. Colmar is also renowned for its art treasures. The Unterlinden museum, which occupies a skilfully-restored former Dominican convent, contains one of the finest examples of early sixteenth-century Rhenish art, the famous Issenheim altar-piece by Mattias Grünewald.

Other typically Alsatian towns include Mulhouse, famed for its textile industry and the possessor of a remarkable museum of printed cloth, and Sélestat with its fine Renaissance town-houses. The houses of Munster, which lies 80 kilometres from Colmar on the road leading to the Col de la Schlucht, are built in a somewhat colder and more severe style than that of other Alsatian towns and display a strong Protestant influence. Munster stands on the Alsatian slopes of the Vosges, steeper and more snowy in winter than those which sweep down to Lorraine. This highland massif is today a playground for the whole of Alsace. Another celebrated area of Alsace is the *ried*, a marshy plain lying between the Rhine and Ill rivers, once a paradise for huntsmen and until recently the haunt of animal-lovers and botanists. This was the last refuge of the famous Alsatian storks and a place where rare orchids grew. Recently it was decided to drain the *ried* and give it over to cereal crops. But this crime against nature aroused passionate protests from all over the world and today the debate on the future of the *ried* is by no means over. The people of Alsace, who cling to the *ried* as part of their heritage, have not yet admitted defeat.

Colmar under snow.

The Lyonnais, Burgundy and Franche-Comté

Ronchamp: chapel of Notre-Dame-du-Haut.

Between the series of barriers separating Western from Central Europe formed by the Jura, the Vosges and the Alps mountain ranges, nature has fashioned a gateway leading to a long corridor. In honour of the province to which they both lead, a province once so important and powerful that it amounted to a State within the State of France, the gateway is known as the "threshold of Burgundy". The gateway, also known as the Belfort Gap, opens out on to Alsace in the east, and Franche-Comté in the west. As for the corridor, it runs south through the Bresse region and the plains of the Saône, skirting Burgundy before reaching the Dombes and the Lyonnais (the region around Lyons) from whence the route to the Mediterranean lies open via the valley of the Rhône.

Around Belfort and Montbéliard, the scenery is somewhat austere and even monotonous, with plateaux, hills, meadows and copses. There are more factory chimneys than church towers and too many armies have passed this way for many historic monuments to have survived. Montbéliard is an important manufacturing centre with its two famous industrial dynasties, the Peugeots and the Japys. Nearby Belfort, today a major centre for the manufacture of electric motors, was once a stronghold commanding its "Gap" between the Vosges and the Jura. Its fort and its ramparts still stand today, along with a famous statue—the Lion of Belfort. This 22-metre-long red granite figure was created by Bartholdi (the sculptor of the Statue of Liberty) to com-

Luxeuil-les-Bains: The House of François I.

memorate the city's heroic resistance against the besieging Prussian army in 1871, when it held out for 103 days and only opened its gates to the enemy on government orders.

Not far from Belfort stands a masterpiece of modern architecture, **the chapel of Notre-Dame-du-Haut at Ronchamp**, built by Le Corbusier in 1955. At the time of its completion traditionalists were shocked by its rough concrete finish and stark lines.

Yet a masterly use of natural light transcends the rough bareness of the stone and lends it a sacred quality. The ancient spa town of **Luxeuil**, 30 kilometres away, is an exception to the general rule in this region, for it contains a number of fine old buildings. Its 6th-century abbey, 18th-century basilica and several ancient dwellings such as **the House of François I** make it a town of exceptional artistic interest.

47

Baume-les-Messieurs.

Water abounds in the Jura. Crystal-clear torrents race downhill through rapids and falls—of which **the Saut du Doubs** (Doubs Falls) is one of the best known—before disappearing underground, only to re-emerge a little further on as innocent streams flowing into some deep, tranquil lake. The Jura holds many attractions for the visitor. It is a paradise for trout and pike fishermen; for hunters in pursuit of the plentiful game in the dense woodland; for skiers who, for four months in the year come to practise every type of skiing imaginable in resorts which have yet to be taken over by the "ski industry".

The highest peaks are in the Central Jura, which is the most frequented area of the range. Here large villages and market towns stand at the entrance to valleys known as "reculées" which penetrate the steep western slopes of the massif. Usually four or five kilometres long, these spectacular blind valleys are walled in by sheer chalk cliffs. The pretty town of Poligny guards the entrance to one such valley; Château-Chalon, famed for its wine, lies at the entrance to another which ends in the lovely mountain amphitheatre known as the Cirque de Ladoye. **Baume-les-Messieurs**, at the head of a valley which leads down to Lons-le-Saunier, is a beautiful village nestling at the foot of another grandiose amphitheatre formed of chalk cliffs. Its inhabitants claim that the two ends of the world meet here, and its labyrinth of grottoes opening out into vast underground halls filled with petrified statues lends some credibility to their claim. Its famous abbey dates from the 15th century. Another lovely valley town in this part of the Jura is Salins-les-Bains, whose saline springs, with the highest mineral content of any in Europe, are a reminder of the distant time when the sea covered the whole of the region.

Franche-Comté, which begins to the south of the Belfort Gap, embraces the greater part of the Jura mountain range. This region, still relatively unspoilt and unaffected by mass tourism, is rich in superb scenery, fine buildings, delicious local produce and spine-chilling legends.

While the mountains of the Vosges are blue, the dominant tone in the Jura is green. Green like the meadows in its foothills, dotted with woods and thickets; green like the forests of conifers, beech and ancient oak trees cloaking its slopes; green like the water of its lakes.

The Doubs Falls.

A cellar at Arbois.

Pérouges: La Rue du Prince.

gave birth to a major industry. Besançon today is France's major watch- and clock-making centre and also, once a year, the scene of an outstanding international music festival.

Music-lovers flock from all over Europe to attend this event, and to admire the lovely city which Victor Hugo once described as "an old Spanish town", alluding to the historic Spanish influence in Franche-Comté. One of its most notable monuments is the magnificent Palais Granvelle, built by Nicolas Perrenot de Granvelle, who grew rich in the service of the Emperor Charles V in the 16th century.

Louis Pasteur was born in the quiet town of Dole, although the great scientist's family home is a few kilometres away in the equally pretty town of **Arbois**, famed for its wine, much appreciated by Henri IV of France.

No account of Franche-Comté would be complete without mentioning its most unusual attraction, Arc-et-Senans. It was here, some 17 kilometres from Salins-les-Bains, that the 18th-century utopian architect Claude Nicolas Ledoux set out to build an ideal city. The factory buildings he erected for the royal saltworks were to be the starting point for a model city which would have been the setting for a perfect society. The effort was remarkable, for while there has been no shortage of utopian writings, utopian architecture is rare. Although purely classical in style, the town planned by Ledoux belongs to the world of fantasy.

The long plain of Bresse stretches out beneath the Jura plateau. Once it was covered with forests so dense and swamps so terrifying that until the 18th century a journey across it was considered as perilous as crossing the Alps. A network of roads has long since tamed its wildness, and today the tender chickens for which Bresse is renowned grow fat in a tranquil, wooded countryside. One magnificent monument that has survived from the days when the province belonged to the dukes of Savoy is **the church of Brou**, less than one kilometre from Bourg-en-Bresse. It dates from the beginning of the 16th century, and it would be hard to imagine any more unbridled expression of the imagination of that epoch.

The Plain of Bresse lies alongside the Dombes, which has fine hunting and fishing. For centuries people here lived from fishing and died from malaria; later they practised a curious form of agriculture, alternately drying out the lakes and sowing the lake beds with crops, then filling the lakes with water again. Today they have reclaimed a good part of the area once and for all, and the climate has grown noticeably healthier.

The Dombes is also worth noting for the town of **Pérouges**, where nearly all the houses date from the Middle Ages or the Renaissance.

A highly individual way of life has grown up in the towns and villages in the valleys. In winter, when the bitter cold prevented the wood-cutters from going out to work in the forests, and when the herds had moved down from their summer pastures, the people for centuries practised cottage industries such as pipe-making, watch- and clock-making. In some cases, as with Besançon, these crafts

The Church of Brou:
Altar-piece in the Chapel
of Margaret of Austria.

Lyons can be disconcerting to the first-time visitor, especially when seen in the fine drizzle or the mist for which the city has a wretched reputation. But it is well worth casting aside preconceived notions and trying, if only for a brief moment, to love Lyons as her citizens do, for the rewards will be more than ample.

The ideal way to begin a tour of Lyons is to climb gently to the top of the Fourvière hill. It is particularly appropriate to start here in fact since this was the site of the ancient Gaulish town of Lugdunum. Two Roman theatres have been excavated at Fourvière, today overlooked by a modern metal tower, as if to remind us that Lyons belongs to the 20th century too.

The summit of the Fourvière offers the best view of the city. Its maze-like topography is psychologically less intimidating than the soulless geometrical layout of many modern cities. Beneath the Fourvière stretches a vista of **roofs with their tall chimneys**, dominated by the twin towers of the Cathedral of Saint-Jean. From here too one can look down on the two rivers that flow together in Lyons, the still-turbulent Rhône and the ever-placid Saône.

Lyons is not an easy city to get to know, and yet she yields herself up to visitors more readily than some are prepared to admit. The ideal thing is to wander through the city at random, until one has seen and taken in everything. But if one is pressed for time, then a little planning is called for. The hill of Croix-Rousse, famous for centuries as the silk-weaving district of Lyons, is well worth a visit. The weavers lived and worked in the old houses of **the Grand-Côte**, at the top of the steps leading to Croix-Rousse. These marvellously skilful craftsmen, working in surroundings where luxury rubbed shoulders with grinding poverty, were also active in

The rooftops of Old Lyons.

Lyons: the Grand-Côte.

the struggle for social justice during the 19th century. "For the great folk of this world fine silks we weave, whilst we, poor weavers, stitchless are laid to earth," runs the song written for them by Aristide Bruant. They toiled from dawn till late at night for a mere pittance, until one day in November 1831 they rose in revolt.

In order to flee the soldiers sent to put down the rebellion, they took refuge in the maze of alleys and stair-cases which are more complex in Croix-Rousse than anywhere else in Lyons. The soldiers, unfamiliar with the city, soon became hopelessly lost

in this inextricable tangle. This maze of narrow streets also played an his-toric role during the Second World War, providing members of the French resistance with a bolt-hole where their safety was virtually guaranteed. It is to these "traboules", as they are known, that Lyons largely owes her place of honour in the an-nals of the French Resistance.

Despite their wretched conditions, the silk-weavers were devoted to their craft. The many examples of their work displayed in Lyons' silk museum, the Maison des Canuts (the French term for the Lyons silk weav-

ers) reveal a high level of accomplish-ment and prove that some of them were great artists. These heroes of the social struggle eventually became legendary popular heroes. In fact they are the main characters in Lyons' version of the Punch and Judy show, which originated in 1808, when a man named Laurent Mourguet created puppet shows based on the lives of the silk-workers of the Croix-Rousse—a world as profound and moving as a play by Brecht.

An evening stroll along the river-side *quais* of Lyons is an enjoyable experience, especially in early au-

53

The Château
de la Rochepot.

tumn when they are at their prettiest. One can go treasure-hunting among the antique shops around the Hôtel de Gadagne, in the old quarter of Saint-Jean, or else walk across the 13th-century La Guillotière bridge to the "chiming peninsula" with its 12 churches. A stroll between the Place Bellecour and the Place des Terreaux, the site of Lyons' splendid town hall, a masterpiece of French civic architecture, offers a variety of opportunities for good eating and drinking. For no visit to Lyons can be considered complete until one has sampled the gastronomic delights for which the city is famous. Celebrated restaurants such as Bocuse have splendidly preserved and even enhanced the reputa-

The vineyards of the Beaujolais.

Chevaliers du Tastevin at Clos-Vougeot.

tion of French cuisine. But Lyons also contains a host of unpretentious taverns where the city's tradition as a centre of simple, wholesome yet subtle good eating is nobly maintained. As for good drinking, some wags even suggest that a third river flows through Lyons—the Beaujolais! In fact the hills of **the Beaujolais** region rise not far from Lyons, thick with sturdy vines. And in Lyons at

least, the wine-lover can be sure that the Beaujolais he drinks is authentic. Any attempt to pass off other wines as Beaujolais would get short shrift from the city's connoisseurs.

The road through the Beaujolais leads through vineyards with fabulous names like Juliénas, Fleurie and Beaujeu, before passing through such Burgundy vineyards as Gevrey-Chambertin, Meursault and Pom-

mard, whose fine growths have made this one of the world's most illustrious wine-growing regions. Each year, in November, the wine sales at the Hospices de Beaune attract crowds of visitors from overseas, with gourmets and shippers rubbing shoulders with diplomats. At some point in the year, each famous vineyard, such as **Clos-Vougeot,** organizes a ceremony at which new initiates are admitted to the Order of **the Chevaliers du Tastevin.**

But Burgundy's reputation does not rest on fine wines alone. She has also managed to preserve a remarkable degree of artistic unity from the days when her dukes reigned, from their seat in Dijon, over a veritable empire stretching from the North Sea to the cantons of Switzerland. Both the lay and the religious architecture of the region bear ample witness to this unity, which makes a distinctive contribution to Burgundy's uniqueness and charm. Humble cottages and splendid châteaux alike are harmoniously proportioned and sturdy.

All are capped with the multi-faceted roofs typical of Burgundy. **The château de la Rochepot** has a magnificent example of this type of roof.

Burgundy was also one of the cradles of Romanesque art, and a wide variety of Romanesque remains have survived there. No fewer than 200 examples have been identified in the Tournus district alone. The abbey of Cîteaux (home of the Cistercian Order) was built in 1098 near Pommard and Mercurey, in the midst of forests and lakes developed and tended by the monks. The Benedictine abbey of Cluny, built in 910, became the intellectual capital of the Christian world in the 11th century.

With its woods and vineyards, rivers and hillsides, châteaux, churches and abbeys, Burgundy extends to the Morvan hills and even includes part of the Paris Basin around the river Yonne, before joining up with the Loire valley. The Morvan possesses at least one architectural gem, **Vézelay,** with its church of the Madeleine, an immense Romanesque edifice with a celebrated tympanum depicting Christ in all his glory. It was here, on 31 May 1146, that St. Bernard preached the Second Crusade. Near **La Charité-sur-Loire,** within the furthest limits of the ancient duchy, the Loire is broader than at any other point, winding through scenery so sublime that down-to-earth Burgundy here ends on an ethereal note.

The Loire at La Charité-sur-Loire.

Vézelay.

Auvergne and the Bourbonnais

The Château de La Bastie d'Urfé: The shell room.

This is a land of lakes, shady forests, viaducts and towns perched like eagles' eyries; Romanesque abbeys built from black laval rock and grey stone; grassy-sloped volcanoes and deep, curving valleys.

The Auvergne is as untameable as a citadel; indeed, it was the fastness of Gaul. It was long the abode of fabulous beasts and craggy-browed peasants; a brooding land where tracks and paths were rarely marked clearly. The Auvergne was a lost land where muleteers could never quite suppress a shudder, for wolves prowled these sunken lanes, spine-chilling legends became shrouded in swirling twilight mists, while the maze-like forest was apt to devour those who ventured beyond its fringes. Even today this region remains untamed, though more prettily so. The tales of wolves and other horrors have been relegated to the cosy fireside. Roads have been constructed, and viaducts flung from one mountain-top to another. The longest viaduct in France, measuring 470 metres, straddles the Sioule River in the Auvergne. In summer, pleasure-craft now ply upon the vast blue lakes that have built up behind the region's massive hydro-electric dams.

But rough, spirited Auvergne can also show the most exquisite breeding when the occasion demands. As early as the 18th century, some of France's most distinguished courtiers paid regular visits to the region's spa towns (which, it is fair to point out, were already known to the ancient Romans) in order to restore their tortured digestive systems, prematurely aged and abused by the sauces and roasts of Versailles. But it was only under the Second

Vichy: the thermal baths.

Empire that the Auvergne truly became a favourite watering place of the upper bourgeoisie. Napoleon III was enchanted by **Vichy** and contributed to its growth.

This rough-hewn yet subtle land also harbours some strangely sophisticated spots, such as **the Château de La Bastie d'Urfé**, built in the 16th century. Here, in a rustic setting, Greek myths mingle with Celtic legends, while the Lignon flows nearby. It was on the banks of this river that Honoré d'Urfé dreamed of the beribboned aristocratic shepherds and shepherdesses that peopled his novel *Astrée*, a voluptuous and bucolic work that enjoyed huge success in the 17th century, though the more prudish salons thought it rather too libertine. The Auvergne can be voluptuous, too, beneath its secretive greenery.

No one can explore this province without falling for one or another of its charms; there is no place for the indifferent among the Auvergne's murmuring brooks and tumultuous petrified lava flows.

Deep in the heart of the massif, the villages cling stubbornly to the volcanic cliffs. Time and the weather have thoroughly harmonized the strong, dark colours that make up this ancient region: greys, blacks and deep blues. Between the Allier and the Dordogne rivers lie rocks and mountains of volcanic origin known as *puys* or *plombs*. The flames that showered from these volcanoes cooled almost at once, creasing the brows of the mountains with colossal furrows. In some places the slopes of the sharply sculpted craters are cloaked with trees and meadows, in others the craters now contain crystal-clear lakes, or, as in the case of **the Puy de Pariou**, a stark new cone has arisen. Man began to inhabit this arid land when the raging volcanoes finally died down, when they had spat their last flaming rocks into the skies and the Auvergne night was chill and silent. Yet the land of the *puys* has never quite shed its prehistoric mantle. Though the smell of sulphur has long since blown away on the wind, the heavy rounded outlines of the mountains are as implacable and powerful as ever.

So the volcanic upheavals subsided but the scars, the wounds and the petrified convulsions all remain outlined against grey horizons. To catch sight of them from the summit of a hill, after a cross-country walk, is a profoundly stirring experience. The grass is scented with valerian and cow-parsnip. Broom and gorse rustle in the wind, bringing a feeling of peace. These mountains are at their best in autumn, when the clouds scud wildly across their peaks and the wind blows in violent squalls, bearing with it the rich scents of vegetation, damp earth, animals and autumn leaves. A majestic melancholy seems to pervade the countryside, and few visitors fail to be affected by it. Everywhere in the Auvergne one is aware of a sense of mystery: it lurks within the woods, keeps watch in every copse, oozes from the peat bogs and blossoms in the meadows of wild thyme and among the hazel trees and honeysuckle.

The people of the Auvergne are tough and sharp-witted. Not so long ago they still settled their disputes with cudgels, always aiming for the head, considered solid enough to withstand a few blows, but never for the legs. They knew from long experience that a man with a few bumps on his skull stands more chance of survival, particularly if he is an awkward customer, than a man with a broken leg. Survival in this harsh environment called for guts and tenacity in the days when it was easy to lose your way on bad roads leading through wild heathland, and when in winter the people laid out their dead on the roofs of their houses to lie buried in snow until spring when they were taken to the cemetery for permanent burial. The Auvergnats have always had to be hard, pugnacious and obstinate. Of course time has worn some of the rough edges off their characters, just as it has worn down the ancient stones of their land. But even today the Auvergnat does not give his friendship easily. He is as direct, as bracing and as suspicious as his country.

The Auvergne has always been poor and remains so to this day. In the past its people lived a withdrawn life in their squat, remote farmsteads. Today many of them have emigrated to other parts of France, attracted by the rewards of big-city life. And yet they return to the Auvergne to spend the last years of their lives in the country where they were born, for the Auvergne is a land that pursues its children wherever they go, inspiring a fierce pride and tenderness. As an anonymous troubadour once sang, long ago in the 13th century: "I've wandered among your sweet-smelling trees, Auvergne, and through your melancholy heathlands. I've glimpsed the heavens in your brooks and streams. And so, proudly I declare today, You are my mother, and you I revere; You are my lover and you I fear."

The Puy de Pariou

The Cantal, lying to the south of the Auvergne mountains, is an enormous collapsed massif, bristling with small volcanic cones (*puys*) and hillocks that spread out into abruptly and bumpily sloping plateaux (known as "planèzes") on whose rough backs grow fields of flax, hemp and fodder-grass, and meadows filled with grazing cattle. Cattle-breeding is the main activity here, and the region is noted for its own breed, the "Salers", with its long curved horns. This powerful, milk-producing strain was developed in the middle of the 19th century by a scientifically-inclined gentleman farmer named Tyssandier d'Escous. There are now 133 head of livestock for every 100 human beings in this region. The cattle spend the winter in stables, where they feed off the provender harvested in the hay meadows. In summer, they go up to the "mountains" to graze, guarded by a few solitary shepherds or herdsmen, who during the season live in primitive huts standing in the middle of the meadows. But the "mountains" in the Auvergne are never all that far from the sturdy-walled farms, which are sometimes found as high up as 1,300 metres.

He who owns cows, in this part of the world, also makes cheese. The best-known cheese of the region is the Cantal; but only the large farms produce enough milk to be able to manufacture it, for it takes 400-500 litres of milk—the produce of more than 20 cows—to make one 50-kilo "fourme" (the traditional name for the large wheel-shaped cheeses made in Cantal). The smaller farmers are more likely to produce the smaller Saint-Nectaire or Bleu d'Auvergne cheeses.

And yet, for all that, this is not a rich land. Until the last century, famine frequently stalked the countryside, and the inactive winter season was long. So people acquired the habit of taking to the roads when the weather turned nasty. They became itinerant chimney-sweeps, cobblers, tinkers, boilermen, door-to-door cloth sales-

The Gorges of the Truyère.

The Château of Anjony.

men, or just plain vagabonds. This seasonal emigration soon spilled over beyond winter, and the people of the Auvergne began to travel the length and breadth of France. They returned to their native land each year, but they ceased to farm their fields, and cultivated land became increasingly rare. Thus many landless peasants were forced to spend half their lives far from their native land. They settled in Paris, selling coal and wood, and sometimes even became hotelkeepers; group feeling remained strong, though, among these exiled people. Nostalgia for the old country is still strong among them today, although once they emigrate, it's usually for good. Those who haven't managed to make their way in the world are too ashamed to return, while those who strike it rich don't want to go back.

To appreciate just how beautiful the mountains they leave behind them are, one just has to contemplate **the Château of Anjony** in its gently rolling valley, or the limpid green waters of **the Gorges of the Truyère**, the quiet scented markets that bring the village squares to life; or again, Romanesque Saint-Nectaire, or southern-flavoured Salers and Laroqueville clinging to its mountainside, huddled around its tiny church that stands between two lime trees. The Cantal should be seen village by village, at the gentle pace of the pedlars of needles, almanachs and tales who wandered through it in former times.

Conques: The reliquary of Sainte Foy.

Between Auvergne, the Cévennes and the Rouergue lie the limestone plateaux known as *Causses*. Trickling streams have eaten their way through the rock, wearing away deep faults. The plateaux are scarred by tragic and splendid abysses, while a surrealistic world built, drop by drop, by the patience of time herself, has grown up at the bottom of *avens* (pot-holes). Inside the Armand *aven* for example, the best known of its kind, a "virgin forest" of 400 stalagmites rises 115 metres beneath the ground. The Dargilan Grotto too, beneath the Causse Noir, is noted for its strange, colourful rock-formations, while above ground, towering over the River Dourbie, at Montpellier-le-Vieux, the wind has sculpted the ruins of a ghost city in the form of weirdly shaped dolomitic rocks.

The Gorges of the Tarn form a gash from one end of the Causses to the other. Over more than 50 kilometres, from Ispagnac to Le Rozier, a canyon more than 500 metres deep divides the Causse de Sauveterre from the Causse Méjean. Ochre cliffs plunge straight down into the foaming emerald waters, while up above the sky is an unblemished blue; the light of Provence bathes the villages here, and their names are redolent of the civilization of Languedoc. **Castelbouc**, for example, stands above the

Peach trees in blossom in the Ardèche.

Castelbouc.

Baumes amphithcatre, while such strangely magnificent spots as Les Vignes and Point Sublîme seem to have been sculpted by some gigantic genius drunk on sunlight.

· Beside the works of nature, those of man are at once more fragile and more moving. One of the finest examples of French Romanesque art is to be found at Conques, some 40 kilometres from Rodez, where the 11th-century church possesses a famous tympanum, bearing a remarkable sculpture of the Last Judgment. It is worth spending at least a day visiting **Conques**, for it is like an encyclopaedia in stone. Also, within its walls lies **the Reliquary of Sainte-Foy**. A ruthless struggle was waged for possession of this pre-Romanesque masterpiece in ancient times. The saint was martyred in 303, in the town of Agen. Her remains were piously preserved, at first in the Church of Sainte-Foy, which grew rich from the stream of pilgrims who came to pay homage. But a jealous and resourceful monk from Conques stole the remains one day. The pil-grims changed direction and headed for Conques and, from that day on, Conques grew prosperous. Far from regarding the theft as a piece of petty larceny, the people of the timc considered it a mighty and even praiseworthy feat, for in the Middle Ages holy relics were not thought of as private property. Like trophies, they belonged to whoever was strong enough or cunning enough to gain possession of them and hang on to them. Conques won them and hung onto them. So, it is within its walls that the richest example of the goldsmith's art in France—a golden, gem-encrusted statue—has dwelt ever since the famous theft.

Towards the east, one loses neither the accents of the Occitan people nor the thousand and one perfumes of a sun-bathed province, but one does gain the blossom-filled light of **the orchards of the Ardèche**. This is almost Provence, and already the ground is thick with highly-scented thyme and lavender.

Seen from the Ardèche, the Rhône looks like a magnificent old lion, roaring in the sunlight. It was along this waterway, 150 years ago, that convicts condemned to be transported were chained in their prison-barges and shipped down-river to Toulon, passing heavily-laden barges painfully struggling upstream. It took ten powerful, steaming horses in harness, all the hauling of the mariners themselves, flailing whips, and the shrill cries of river children to haul one of these barges against the strong current.

Sometimes the chains would snap, and the boats would founder like great vessels on the ocean. Those days are now long past; the river has been tamed, and people no longer sing of the saga of the Rhône.

Yet these towns have all retained an irresistible and tender old-world charm, the kind one can feel among the old dwellings of Serrières at mid-day, listening to the chink of china-ware through the open windows, and to the sound of simple crafts. One should pause a while to sit in the shade of the almost Italianate porch of the church at Andance, or linger for some time in Tournon, in whose school Mallarmé studied, and in whose château Ronsard lived. One should sip the spirited wines of Cornas or Saint-Péray; and no stay in the region is complete without a visit to **Crussol**, perched on its mountain top like an immovable sentinel.

There is a superb maelstrom of rocks and thornbushes as one rises away from the valley. We come now to the Amphitheatre of Rochemaure and the Forest of Païolive—a forest of stone peopled with sprites—before following the course of the Gorges of the Ardèche, as steep as the Gorges of the Tarn. Millions of years ago the river bored a 60-metre arch in the rock—**the Pont d'Arc**—before pursuing its southward course, drawn irresistibly by the magnet of the sun.

The Château of Crussol.
The Ardèche at the Pont d'Arc.

7

Savoy and Dauphiné

The birth of the Alps must have been a fantastic sight, far more impressive than any science-fiction film: the earth's crust rears skywards and cracks apart in a series of mighty convulsions; the rocks crumble and burst open to form yawning abysses; titanic waves of rock move inexorably forward like a glacier to engulf a whole region. Geologists are still arguing about when and why the Alps came into being, but on one point they all agree: the Alps as we know them are only the remains of a far higher mountain range and if erosion had not taken place their peaks would tower tens of thousands of metres into the sky.

The Alps today form a mountain range 300 kilometres long and 150 kilometres wide, much of it in France. Their highest mountain, Mont Blanc, dominates the whole European continent from its 4,807-metre-high summit. Oddly enough, as Hannibal's elephants proved long ago, the Alps have never formed an impassable barrier owing to the valleys, depressions and small plains which intersperse the mountains. Man settled in the Alpine region early in history, but for many centuries few people apart from shepherds and hunters ever ventured high up the mountain slopes. Today mountains like the Alps fascinate us partly because they afford a glimpse of natural beauty unsullied by human interference, but until the 18th century they were regarded with something akin to horror and thought to be haunted by demons. It was the cult of nature launched by Rousseau and the early Romantics that made the world sensitive to the beauty of high mountains. The first ascent of Mont Blanc, made by Balmat and Paccard, both from Chamonix, in 1786, dates from this period. The second ascent was made the following year by the Swiss scholar De Saussure. Nineteenth-century Romantics such as Shelley, Goethe and Hugo also came under the spell of the Alps and during the same period the word "alpinist" was coined to denote a person who feels the strange need to push himself to the limit and master his fears in order to scale a mountain. Today the whole region is a vast holiday playground for the French people. But dotted with ski resorts and crisscrossed with cable railways though they may be, the Alps still provide a refuge for those in search of solitude, for those who cannot resist the challenge to pit themselves against nature, and for those who want to enjoy unspoiled natural beauty.

Climbing the Gros Rognon.

Cable railway on the Aiguille du Midi.

The Aiguille du Plan.

71

Ibexes in the Vanoise national park.

The Alps are a world unto themselves, containing almost every kind of geological formation: small plains like the Grésivaudan, river basins like that of the Arve, broad valleys, narrow gorges, lakes, plateaux, gentle slopes, steep slopes, high pastureland, towering peaks, glaciers and eternal snows.

The southern Alps have a dry Mediterranean climate, the northern Alps are wet and cool. On the mountain slopes and in the pastureland and forests grows a vast variety of flowers and plants. And until the hunters took their toll, many animals flourished there too.

In the central part of the Alps, the mountain uplands are grouped around the Maurienne, Oisans and Tarentaise valleys, where the big ski resorts are located. Here determined efforts have been made to preserve the flowers and animals and other aspects of natural beauty imperilled by indiscriminate hunting. The entrance to the Tarentaise valley, near Conflans, is difficult of access, but further on it opens out, green and peaceful. This remote valley, where the women still wear, on special occasions, their fine traditional costumes and exquisite headdresses, leads to the Vanoise national park. This nature reserve,

which lies 2,000 metres above sea level, was created in 1963 as an extension of the Grand Paradis park across the frontier in Italy, which dates from the beginning of the century. One-fifth of the park is covered with snow and ice. It provides protection for all the plants and animals threatened with extinction within its 60,000-hectare area: flowers that thrive in an Arctic climate; rare birds such as the ptarmigan; and animals threatened or driven from their habitat by the ubiquitous skiers. One such animal is the nimble Alpine **ibex**, a small animal about a metre high, with horns in some cases the same length, which resembles the chamois of the Pyrenees. Other animals whose future hung in the balance have also taken refuge in the Grand Paradis and Grande Vanoise parks. They include hazel grouse and marmots, black grouse, hares, badgers, martens and foxes who flourish in this high-altitude Eden, where they can sun themselves peacefully on the rocks far from the hunter's threat.

Visitors are allowed in the Vanoise park, provided they respect the rules, the most important of which is to leave the animals absolutely alone.

heard is the song of birds, the murmuring of insects, the sighing of the wind and the splashing of waterfalls and swift-flowing rivers. In the cool, rarefied air one feels overwhelmed with joy and energy. The atmosphere of peace floods the mind with a feeling of power, making sustained physical effort seem far easier than down in the valley. Even when darkness falls, the hum of life continues and the park is never completely silent. In fact dusk is the best time of day to appreciate what an untamed mountain paradise can be like. It is a lost world

where the visitor can rediscover his inner self and appreciate his true place in the universe, as a minute human presence beneath the stars in an indifferent world. The thousand small noises of the park at night reinforce this impression: the fluttering wings and startled cry of a bird; the sighing of the wind.

The visitor to the Grande Vanoise park can continue his peaceful, meditative journey in the south of the park, passing through **the Col de l'Izoard**, which leads towards the sunshine and cloudless skies of the Mediterranean. The beauty of the Col assumes a noble, imperious quality when the snow transforms its serried ranks of fir-trees into sparkling sculptures. And yet the world of men is not so far away: houses and settlements cluster around the many lakes which soften the rugged beauty of these mountainous uplands—**the lake of Serre-Ponçon**, the lake of Annecy, and Lake Geneva, the biggest of the Alpine lakes. Their mysterious waters shimmer in so many different lights that they seem to be made of completely different layers of water, each with its own texture. Yet they all create around themselves the same atmosphere of calm and serenity.

On the road to the Col de l'Izoard.

The way to approach Vanoise is from Modane to the south, passing through the town of Lanslebourg and the Col de l'Iseran. The park is a huge garden luxuriant with rare and beautiful flowers such as the glacier crowfoot, gentian, aquilegia, spring anemone, edelweiss and the simple yet delicate myosotis. The only way to see the park is on foot, but this is no hardship. Paths wind through the woods among grasses and flowers, alongside gurgling streams and rocks still white from the night frosts. The light is extraordinarily clear and bright. High up in this reserve of wild life, nature and peace, all that can be

The Lake of Serre-Ponçon.

The chapel of Notre-Dame-de-Toute-Grâce:
stained glass window by Rouault.

The northern French Alps attract more tourists—whether climbers, skiers, hikers or those in search of relaxation in the mountain air—than their southern counterparts. As well as being better endowed with hotels and ski-lifts, they are more grassy, more thickly wooded, more welcoming in summer and more snowy in winter.

This region contains some of France's most important and renowned spa towns, such as Evian and Aix-les-Bains. Evian, which specializes in the treatment of kidney diseases and obesity, markets 350 million bottles a year of the water whose health-giving properties first won the town its reputation. Another important source of tourist revenue is its casino, open all the year round. At Aix, today France's third most important spa, people have taken the waters since Roman times.

The Oisans valley is the starting-point for three classic ascents—to the summits of the Meije, the Écrins and the massif of the Grandes Rousses—while Chamonix has been famed among mountaineers since the end of the 18th century. Mont Blanc still challenges climbers and also intrepid skiers who ski on the glaciers which stretch down from its central ice dome. Ski resorts abound, old and new, big and small. Some of the most important are the charming town of Megève; Courchevel, for many years the winter equivalent of Saint-Tropez; sunny Meribel; and Avoriaz, whose modern concrete buildings have been designed to harmonize with their mountainous setting. The visitor who is willing to go off the beaten track can still discover for himself villages which have not been taken over by the winter sports industry.

In the valley of the Arly, for example, are villages where there are traditional chalets and cafés with wooden counters where one can drink elbow-to-elbow with the Savoyards the delicious sharp white wine of Savoy. In the days before antibiotics were discovered for the treatment of tuberculosis, large numbers of sanatoria were built on these healthy mountain slopes. There are many in the region around Saint-Gervais-les-Bains, which is both a winter sports resort and a centre for the treatment of skin diseases. But on the Plateau of Assy, not far from Chamonix, amateurs of modern art today outnumber invalids, for this is the site of the famous church of **Notre-Dame-de-Toute-Grâce**. Built between 1937 and 1950, the church was decorated by some of the greatest French painters of that period. Fernand Léger created a vast mosaic for the entrance, Henri Matisse and Georges Rouault designed the windows, and Braque and Bonnard were among the other contributors.

Paradoxically enough, there are perhaps more diversions in the northern French Alps during the summer months than in winter. When the snows have melted and the skiers have gone, sightseers begin to arrive in their thousands for less strenuous pursuits. A wide range of excursions can be made: one can climb by train from Montenvers to see the Mer de Glace, the immense 45-square-kilometre stretch of perpetually frozen ice that forms Mont Blanc's biggest glacier, or be hoisted to **the Aiguille du Midi** (see page 71) by the world's highest cable railway (3,842 metres), or even try the ascent of Mont Blanc itself. In June and July the park of La Vanoise and **the Alpine Garden of le Lautaret** are at their best and most fragrant. The latter, which stands on the edge of the southern Alps, has 2,000 varieties of flowers and commands a magnificent view over the massif of the Pelvoux.

The Alpine garden of the Lautaret.

Country road in the Vercors.

Savoy has only been French since 1860. Before that it had a checkered history for hundreds of years as a kind of football in the European power game. It passed from the kingdom of Sardinia to France during the French Revolution then went back to Sardinia after Napoleon's downfall. Finally it was ceded to France as a reward for French aid in Italy's war against Austria in 1859, to the satisfaction of its people, who voted almost unanimously in favour of returning to France in a plebiscite held in 1860. Dauphiné, on the other hand, its southern neighbour, has been part of France since the 14th century when its ruler, the dauphin Humbert II, sold it to Charles V of France for 200,000 crowns. The word dauphin, originally a personal name, was borne so frequently by the medieval rulers of the Viennois, the nucleus of the province of Dauphiné, that they took it as their title. As part of the deal, Humbert stipulated that the heir-apparent to the French throne should henceforth bear the title of dauphin, and the practice began whereby French kings ceded the Dauphiné to their heirs. Grenoble, the ancient capital of Dauphiné, has a great reputation for dynamism. It was a pioneer in promoting tourism, and in 1889 became the first French city to create a local tourist board (syndicat d'initiative). In 1968 it was host to the Winter Olympics. In the pleasant countryside around the city there are some fine chateaux and manor-houses, one of which, Vizille,

played an important role in French history. It was at Vizille on 14 June 1788 that the provincial estates of Dauphiné demanded the convocation of the Estates-General, which was to spark off the French Revolution of 1789.

Towering above Grenoble are the white rocks and sombre forests of **the plateau of the Vercors**, cleft with deep gorges through which the river Bourne rushes to join the Isère. This peaceful region where the Mediterranean climate already begins to be felt, was the scene of bitter fighting in June and July 1944. Grenoble and its surrounding hills were the seat of some of the most active French resistance groups, and here in the Vercors some 4,000 partisans perished after defying several German divisions. Their heroic stand is today commemorated by a monument on the plateau.

The French Alps have been through two revolutions since the days when their economy was predominantly agricultural. The first was an industrial revolution which began with the exploitation of hydro-electric power. The second, much more important and far-reaching, has been the tourist revolution that has changed the face of the region and its pattern of life. But some places are impervious to "tourist pollution", and one of them is undoubtedly **the Grande Chartreuse** founded in 1084 by St. Bruno. One of the world's most famous monasteries, it is situated in a rocky fold of the Alps near Grenoble.

The Grande Chartreuse.

Provence and Languedoc

A paradise of olive trees and cypresses perched high on a hillside. Here and there among the trees and flowers stand pieces of sculpture looking so completely at home in their setting that it would be impossible to imagine the landscape without them. Masterpieces of modern painting hang in a spacious, airy building nearby, where five rooms are devoted to the works of Braque, Kandinsky, Chagall, Miro and Giacometti. This is **the Maeght Foundation** at Saint-Paul-de-Vence, one of the most remarkable living museums in the world.

Orange and lemon trees, pine-trees, pale rocks tumbling chaotically down to the glittering turquoise sea below. The only sounds are the murmur of the wind and waves and the song of the crickets. The scent of warm rock and pine-resin rises in the nostrils. This is **the peninsula of Saint-Jean-Cap-Ferrat**, where the bustle, the crowds and traffic jams of Nice seem far away.

France's Mediterranean coast is a very special place. Its natural beauty and brilliant light have fascinated many painters, among them Picasso who died at Mougins, inland from Cannes, and Renoir who spent his old age at Cagnes. The château Gri-

The Maeght Foundation at Saint-Paul-de-Vence.

Saint-Jean-Cap-Ferrat.

maldi at Cagnes is now a museum of Picasso's works, and nearby at Vallauris is the pottery centre he encou-raged. Public opinion polls have shown that 70 per cent of French people would live in Provence or on the Côte d'Azur if they had the choice. A sizeable percentage of the rest of Europe seems to feel the same

Nice.

along the seafront which is still called the Promenade des Anglais. Here stand great luxury hotels and extravagant rococo villas constructed during the "Belle Époque" by aristocrats and adventurers for whom money was no object. They look out across the Promenade to the cobalt panorama of the Mediterranean, the Baie des Anges stretching westwards to the Cap d'Antibes. The Baie, usually thronged with pleasure boats, presents a breath-taking sight from the top of the Rocher du Château, which also commands a fine view of the charming old district of Nice, with its narrow old houses as brightly-coloured as children's paintings. Narrow old streets and alleys twist and turn between tiny squares and steep flights of steps. The fruit, herb and flower markets teem with life and good humour, as bantering comments fly back and forth, often made in the old Nice dialect.

But perhaps even more enchanting are the sleepy little towns in the hills of the *arrière-pays*. The houses cling stubbornly to the steep hills and huddle tightly together as though looking for mutual protection against the fierce gusts of the Mistral. In this

way, judging from the thousands of people who make for this stretch of coastline each year in search of the sun and the good life. The scenery is beautiful and the climate exceptionally mild, with temperatures averaging 22° in summer and rarely dropping below 10° in winter. The region also gets an average of 3,000 hours of sunshine a year.

A vast holiday playground stretches from the Italian frontier to the Rhône delta, from the Riviera (first christened the Côte d'Azur in 1887) to the massifs of the Esterel and the Maures. There are countless towns, villages and ports to explore on the coast and in the upland areas of the *arrière-pays* or hinterland. The big difficulty is to know where to start. For those who like towns, **Nice** is the place, with its picturesque, animated processions and festivals such as the famous Mardi Gras carnival. Founded in 350 B.C. by members of the Greek colony at Marseilles, who

named it Niké—"victory"—Nice was a major port until the 18th century. By the early 19th, it was already starting to attract English tourists during the winter. It was they who laid out the 7-kilometre-long promenade

Saint-Tropez.

world of steep mountain cliffs, olive groves and vineyards, flower-decked hillsides and rolling plains, these ancient hill towns jut out like jagged crowns on their hilltops, their shady narrow streets bordered by houses with pink, yellow, grey and white facades and tiled roofs of pink or ochre. As well as a maze of streets, many of them, such as **Tourette-sur-Loup**, still have a rectangular square, once a Roman forum.

Before it became a fashionable resort, **Saint-Tropez**, at the foot of the Maures uplands, was a fishing village. Before that it was a pirate stronghold. In summer the crowds take it over, following in the well-trodden footsteps of the stars who made it famous. Fortunately, the old houses packed together within the ramparts have left little room for new building, and so it is still possible to see Saint-Tropez as painters and writers like Colette saw it—but only in the autumn, when the summer visitors have gone.

Tourette-sur-Loup.

Lavender field near Castellane.

From the Esterel massif a long chain of famous resorts stretches east as far as the Italian frontier. In some of them luxury villas and hotels are now mixed with resort facilities of a more popular kind—holiday villages and caravan sites; others still aim to attract the wealthy. Sainte-Maxime, today somewhat overshadowed by nearby Saint-Tropez, belongs very definitely in the second category and inclines towards opulent holiday homes rather than tents or caravans. A different atmosphere reigns at Cavalaire-sur-Mer, which gives onto a 10-kilometre-long beach of white sand curving round a pleasant bay sheltered from the wind. Here extensive camp sites and thousands of modest villas intersperse the oleanders and pine trees. All along the coast between the Giens peninsula and Cannes vivid porphyry hills clothed with cork oaks and pines plunge almost sheer into the sea. For the moment the building promoters are still drooling over the possibilities of the Giens peninsula, near Hyères, but fortunately the lovely offshore islands of Port-Cros, Porquerolles and the Ile du Levant now seem to be permanently protected from "development" Further east are Saint-Raphael, fashionable ever since it was launched in the 19th century by Alexandre Dumas and the journalist-pamphleteer Alphonse Karr, and Fréjus, which was built by Caesar and has a Roman amphitheatre.

The eastern end of the Côte d'Azur is dominated by Nice and Cannes. The popularity of Cannes dates from 1834 when Lord Brougham decided to stay there because a cholera epidemic was raging in his customary resort of Nice. He came back regularly for 30 years. From Nice a three-tiered system of roads known as the Corniches runs to Monte Carlo and then on to the Italian frontier. The highest, the Grande Corniche, was built by Napoleon to replace a Roman road. Facing Nice across the Baie des Anges is the walled town of Antibes, a resort whose star is rising among the kind of people who made the reputation of Saint-Tropez a few years ago. The annual festival of traditional jazz at Juan-les-Pins, next door, has become world famous. The scent of orange blossom seems always to hang in the air at Menton, the last French resort before the Italian frontier, which is noted even on the Côte d'Azur for its exceptionally mild climate.

For the visitor who has taken his fill of sun and the sybaritic pleasures of the coast, a more invigorating atmosphere and more rugged scenery lie waiting in the mountainous *arrière-pays,* which is perhaps also more beautiful. Above Cannes, near Castellane, the road leads upwards to the Alps through a parched, empty landscape. In summer the scent of lavender, the only crop that will grow on this dry soil, wafts gently over **the lavender fields** on gusts of warm wind. Here **the Verdon** river flows through a 1,000-metre-deep canyon which is one of France's most spectacular scenic beauties. In the *arrière-pays,* with its mountains and arid fields, its plateaux and gorges, its pine trees, lavender and sheep, Provence shows a face that is brutally hard. Water is unpredictable, subterranean. Either it is absent altogether or it springs violently out of cracks in the chalk, its presence marked by greenery and in the villages by a blossoming of fountains.

The gorges of the Verdon.

Toulon.

The Queen of Arles.

The *calanque* of Morgiou.

Wild bulls of the Camargue.

The amphitheatre at Arles.

The Côte d'Azur is Provence's glittering showcase, but it is only one aspect of this sun-drenched region. Between the Riviera and the Rhône delta there is another Provence, less cosmopolitan and less hectic than the coast but just as beautiful and more deeply rooted in the soil. It begins at the seaport and naval base of **Toulon**, whose old quarters are particularly attractive.

Further west along the coast beyond Bandol, **calanque** country begins. The *calanques,* most of which lie in the few miles of coastline between Marseilles and the picturesque fishing port of Cassis, are spectacular mini-fiords that bite deep into the white cliffs and then extend inland in the form of dry, rugged valleys. These jagged fiord-sides whose harsh grandeur is softened only by the pines and shrubs clinging to them rise almost sheer from the sea, forming an impressive and still relatively little-known sight. Yachtsmen anchor in some of them; rock-climbers scale others; they all offer an escape to solitude and peace.

For many of those who love Provence, the fine old town of Arles epitomizes the province more than any other place. It has a spectacular setting : on one side stretches the marshy plain of the Camargue, on the other rise the Alpilles hills. On the Alpilles side lovely villages nestle among olive trees, sheltering from the Mistral in folds of the ground. They have names like Saint-Rémy-de-Provence, Saint-Michel, Barbentane, Mouriès and Font-vieille, where Alphonse Daudet wrote his *Letters from my Mill.* Perched atop a craggy rock formation is the ancient village of Les-Baux-de-Provence, where each Christmas a renowned church service is held to resemble the first Christmas. Nearby stands the fine 12th-century abbey of Montmajour, with its Romanesque crypts and cloister. On the seaward side of Arles, between the mouths of the Grand Rhône and the Petit Rhône, the Camargue extends in stretches of pastureland and marsh, dotted with clusters of houses and an occasional *mas* (big farm) sheltered from the Mistral by a curtain of trees. The only real town on the Camargue is Saintes-Maries-de-la-Mer, twice a year the centre of a gypsy pilgrimage. Part of the Camargue has been made into a nature reserve to protect its unique flowers and animal life, including its famous pink flamingoes. Elsewhere rice-growing has transformed the Camargue economy. But traditions die hard and herds of **wild bulls** can still be seen, tended by cowboys mounted on tough little Camargue horses.

Arles is a truly exceptional town not only by virtue of its setting but through its history, its monuments and its atmosphere. Its many Roman remains include public baths, temples, a theatre, one of the most celebrated cemeteries of the Roman period, the Alyscamps (Elysii Campi), and **a stone amphitheatre** today regularly used in the summer for bullfights. The church of Saint-Trophime has a set of extremely beautiful cloisters decorated with remarkable stone carvings of Biblical scenes. In the 15th century the Knights Templars built the Priory beside the Rhône which today houses the Réattu Museum. Each July this mysterious, secretive, exciting town holds a carnival presided over by **the Queen of Arles**, who must look like a true Arlesienne, own an authentic folk costume, know all there is to know about the town's traditions, and speak Provençal.

Marseilles: the old port.

It is impossible to know how far the beauty of the towns and villages of Provence is due to the beauty of their natural setting. All one can say is that in some elusive way a perfect harmony seems to have evolved between these human settlements and the Provençal landscape. Arles is one example of this harmony. Aix, which some claim to be the most beautiful town in France, is another. Unlike Arles, Aix does not possess any important Roman remains although it has many ancient buildings and fine old houses. The capital of Provence during the Middle Ages, it became a brilliant intellectual centre during the reign of René of Provence in the 15th century. In the 17th and 18th, it was transformed into the ordered, harmonious town we can see today by the Counts of Provence and members of the Provençal *parlement* (which had sat at Aix since its creation in 1501) who built mansions, pavilions, gardens and squares with ornamental fountains. Their work can be seen at its best in the dignified houses on the Cours Mirabeau, the avenue lined with plane trees which is the main centre of life in Aix. These aristocratic *hôtels particuliers* are superb examples of classical architecture whose solemnity has melted away beneath the Provence sun. Aix has been a university town since the 15th century, and today as the seat of the Aix-Marseilles university is one of the biggest university centres in France. A more recent institution is the Aix music festival, now world famous.

Aix shares its university with its turbulent neighbour **Marseilles**, chief seaport of southern France and the country's second largest city. Through its history, its culture, its topography and its spirit, Marseilles is an enclave of the Hellenic tradition in France. The modern city stands on the site of the colony of Massilia, founded by

Marketing in Marseilles.

Greek sailors and merchants from Phocaea in Asia Minor around 600 B.C. (although it is probable that Phoenicians had settled there even earlier). This makes Marseilles the oldest city in France. Recent excavations beneath the Place de la Bourse have revealed traces of the earliest port installations and shown that Marseilles rapidly became a thriving town and trading centre. Since then the city has grown like some irrepressible climbing plant over the hills and valleys around the port.

Marseilles has always been a lively, cosmopolitan city, and a good place to taste its exotic, exuberant atmosphere is in **the markets around the old port**. This is also an opportunity to taste a good piquant **bouillabaisse**, the famous fish stew containing red mullet, the *rascasse* and other Mediterranean fish, plus tomatoes, onions, herbs, olive oil and garlic seasoning. Savour the dish and soak in the atmosphere. Somebody is bound to be telling a long, involved, epic story, never using one word when ten will do. Among their other qualities the *Marseillais* are terrific raconteurs.

Bouillabaisse

The interior of Provence between the Rhône and the Alps is just as beautiful and has quite as much to offer as the coast. Its towns, such as Orange, Avignon, Vaison-la-Romaine, are beautiful and set in a landscape of **fields fringed with cypress trees**. The light is that of an Italian primitive. Visit Manosque and Forqualier in the Durance valley and you will find many reminders of the 19th-century Provençal poet Frédéric Mistral and the modern novelist Jean Giono whose works are set in Provence. Go to Carpentras and drink *pastis* beneath the lime trees, then climb the slopes of Mont Ventoux above the town. Explore the Luberon mountains and scale the 1800-metre-high Signal de Lure above Saint-Étienne-les-Orgues. Don't miss the charming town of L'Isle-sur-la-Sorgue and the Fontaine de Vaucluse nearby, where the Sorgue river surges up from its underground channel. Another impressive sight is the old village of Gordes not far away, its tightly packed houses huddling 275 metres up on a

A *borie* at Gordes.

rocky spur. It has a 16th-century château which is now a museum of the work of the Op Art painter Vasarely. A little further on, along the Sénancole valley, a narrow road leads to the Cistercian abbey of Sénanque, founded in 1148. Its well-preserved buildings today house a research centre for Saharan studies. Here is a parched landscape of the oak-forested hills known as *garrigues* and dazzling boulder-strewn hillsides with a riot of vegetation occasionally marking the course of a stream or river.

Here and there along the country roads one comes across curious drystone buildings known as **bories**. Sometimes round, sometimes rectangular, they are roofed with slabs of limestone traditionally known as *lauzes*. The origins of these primitive buildings are obscure, but it has been suggested that they may date back to prehistoric times. Their vaulted roofs are reminiscent, though on a smaller scale, of the tombs of Mycenaean Greece. The shepherds of Haute Provence always used them as shelters on their annual trek to the high pastures, and it has been suggested that plague-victims used them as refuges.

Fields in the Rhône valley.

Vineyards of Languedoc.

Nîmes: the Maison Carrée.

West of the Rhône delta is Languedoc, **an expanse of vineyards** stretching inland from sandy beaches. In the past these vineyards were Languedoc's main economic asset, but today the wine-growers find themselves obliged to diversify in order to survive. The sandy beaches, on the other hand, have become an El Dorado. In 1965 the French government decided on an ambitious project to promote and develop the holiday potential of the most desolate part of the coastline, then little more than mosquito-infested marshland plus a few tiny resorts patronized by holidaymakers from Arles, Nîmes and Montpellier. Today the project is a reality. Boldly-designed towns and harbours have been built to form leisure zones such as La Grande Motte (designed by the urbanist-architect Georges Candilis), Port-Barcarès and Port-Leucate, where everything is laid on for holidaymakers, except perhaps the atmosphere and sense of community which only a long history can give. But not far away is **Nîmes**, which has both. Nîmes, which stands at the foot of a chain of barren hills, the Monts Garrigues, is as elegant as its traditional rival, Arles, and has the same abundance of Roman remains, but it is less warm and expansive. A strong Protestant tradition has imbued Nîmes with a more placid atmosphere than one might expect to find in the Mediterranean world. There are extensive Roman remains in this essentially 18th-century town. The **Maison Carrée**, a temple dating from the time of the Emperor Augustus (Ist century B.C.), is one of the finest monuments to have survived in the old Roman province of Gaul. Among the other Roman remains at Nîmes are an amphitheatre, the best-preserved in France and now used for bullfights, and the Tour Magne, a ruined Roman tower which is the oldest monument in Nîmes and was once used as a watch-tower before being turned into a fortress by the medieval Counts of Toulouse. Each Whitsuntide bullfighting buffs from all over France converge on Nîmes for the "corridas", and for three days the staid town erupts into a frenzy of enjoyment to the accompaniment of brass bands and fireworks.

Perhaps more enjoyable than big occasions of this kind are the smaller village bullfights where the atmosphere is equally gay and spontaneous. Almost every Sunday in summer there are village fêtes in the Nîmes, Arles, Sète, Montpellier, Béziers and Narbonne area, with competitions in which *razeteurs,* men dressed in white and equipped with a small metal rake attached to their knuckles, compete in snatching a ribbon from between a bull's horns. Towns such as Arles, Saintes-Maries-de-la-Mer and **Aigues-Mortes** with its light stone **ramparts** preserve the tradition of letting bulls loose in the streets. On carnival day cowboys drive the bulls through barricaded streets, while local heroes try to provoke the animals to force the cowboys to show off their skills.

A fête beneath the ramparts of Aigues-Mortes.

Corsica

Corsica is an island of sudden contrasts and infinite variety. Here a mountain rises vertically out of the sea; there a peninsula points a finger to the mainland of France. Inland there is the undergrowth of the *maquis,* fragrant with thyme, laurel, rosemary and wild flowers; dark, gloomy forests of oak, pine and chestnut trees; undulating lines of green hills and snowy mountains, culminating in the 2,700-metre-high Mount Cinto, where the skiing season lasts until May. And perhaps most spectacular of all there is the Corsican coastline with its secret magic coves and rocky, porphyry-red cliffs.

The third largest island in the Mediterranean, Corsica is 180 kilometres south of the Côte d'Azur and only 80 kilometres from the Italian coast. The island of Sardinia lies to the south. "Everything was better and more beautiful there", Corsica's most famous son, Napoleon Bonaparte, used to say nostalgically as he thought back to his childhood days on the island. If you approach Corsica from the sea, its charm starts to work even before you set foot on its shores. The salty, seaweed tang of the open sea gives way to the offshore breeze bearing with it a unique combination of fragrant perfumes that is typically Corsican: a mixture of aloe-wood and juniper, cistus and asphodel, eucalyptus and lentisk, lavender and myrtle.

The best place to begin to discover this enchanting island is the wild and unspoilt Sartene in the southern part of Corsica. Here the granite mountains, cleft by dramatic gorges, plunge down into the sea, forming spectacular white cliffs. Filitosa on the coast is the major site of proto-historic monuments in Corsica. Fortifications and dolmens dating back to the second pre-Christian millenium have been discovered; today they are as much a part of the natural landscape as the green hills and pine trees. At the southernmost tip of the island is **Bonifacio**, poised spectacularly on a promontory of white cliffs and unchanged in its essentials since the 13th century. The promontory on which the town is built runs parallel with the mainland, separated by a creek which forms a harbour lined with cafés and restaurants. The citadel on the hill was built in 829 by a Tuscan noble, Boniface, to protect the town from Saracen invasions. The building has survived 11 centuries absolutely unchanged; even the drawbridge which links the citadel to the outside world is original.

Bonifacio.

The beach at Palombaggia.

The *calanches* of Piana.

All over Corsica fortresses and citadels bear silent witness to the island's long and bloody history. Throughout the centuries it has been bitterly fought over, relentlessly invaded and doggedly defended. Corsica's recorded history begins in 560 B.C. when Greeks from Phocaea in Asia Minor founded the town of Alalia on the east coast. Then came the Etruscans, who were in turn followed by the Romans, the Saracens, the Pisans, the Genoans and even, at one stage, Muslim pirate chiefs. In 1736 a German adventurer, Theodor von Neuhof, landed with a shipload of arms and persuaded the Corsican leaders to proclaim him king. He remained on the island for a year until he ran out of funds and had to leave. But the rebellion against Corsica's Genoese masters continued without him, and the French were asked for help in suppressing it. At this stage the Corsican national hero Pascal Paoli appeared on the scene. He liberated the island and organized it democratically, but only for the short space of 14 years. In 1768 the Genoans sold their rights in Corsica to France and the French invaded the island, defeating the patriots at Ponte Nuovo in May 1769, and Paoli fled to England. Some months later, on August 15, Napoleon Bonaparte was born in Ajaccio.

All these many occupations have left enduring traces behind them. **Bastia**, the island's biggest city and major commercial centre, is a Genoan city. An enclave within

Genoese bridge at Ota Spelunca.

Bastia, the citadel (Bastiglia) which gave the city its name dominates the old port with its two jetties. Apart from the Palais des Gouverneurs, there are few outstanding monuments in Bastia, which owes its charm to other factors: the vaulted passages and twisting alleys of its old quarters, its cool squares and its plain white buildings.

The Genoese have also left their mark on the little seaside town of Saint-Florent nestling at the western base of Cap Corse. One could easily transpose **Saint-Florent** with its network of canals to a pretty Adriatic island such as Torcello. Here and there in Corsica one comes across other traces of the Genoese presence in the form of beautifully-curved but fragile-looking bridges. A particularly fine **Genoese bridge** is the one at Ota Spelunca near Porto on the west coast.

Though Corsica abounds in picturesque reminders of its checkered past, its natural beauty equals its man-made attractions. One outstanding scenic beauty, the Gulf of Porto Vecchio on the south-east coast is virtually an inland sea hemmed in by **the Palombaggia peninsula**. It has glorious beaches of golden sand, blue skies and a sea whose colour changes from green to blue as the sun runs its course. On the other side of the island is one of Corsica's most astonishing sights, **the calanches of Piana**, 300-metre-high red rock pinnacles.

The *maquis*.

Saint-Florent.

Bastia: a street in the old town.

The Col de Bavella.

The road out of Porto-Vecchio twists and turns up the steep mountainside into a dense, fragrant pine forest, the Forêt de l'Ospedale, a place of savage splendour where huge rocks rear up like fortresses between the trees. Far away in the distance Sardinia can be seen across the sea. The forest continues as high as **the Col de Bavella**, over 1,200 metres above sea level. Below the Col lies a valley ringed with almost vertical mountainsides; above rises a range of sawn-off, dentate peaks, glowing in the sunshine.

The road through these mountain fastnesses winds upwards in a series of narrow hairpin bends through high passes such as the Col de la Vaccia, the Col de la Verde and the Col de Corba and occasional isolated villages like Ghisoni. There are occasional dizzying glimpses of the chaos of pine trees and tumbled rocks below and panoramic views over the surrounding countryside. At last the town of Corte appears in the distance, sheltering behind its reputedly impregnable ramparts high on a rocky peak. The historic capital of central Corsica, Corte was the seat of Pascal Paoli's government during his short rule over the island between 1755 and 1769. It is an austere, slightly melancholy town with a great deal of charm and atmosphere. Around it stretches Corsica's park and nature reserve with the beautiful Tavignano and Restonica gorges and two lakes, Melo and Capitello, almost 2,000 metres high. They are dominated by the rocky pinnacle of Mount Rotondo, at 2,600 metres Corsica's second highest mountain.

Descending towards the rocky north-west coast, the road passes through Ile

Rousse and Calvi, the latter on a superb site looking out over a bay. Against its mountainous backdrop, Calvi has a citadel surrounded by little old houses, animated quayside life and a long beach of golden sand. Between the low hills of Ile Rousse and the rugged mountain landscape of the interior lies the gentle inland plain of La Balagna, fertile and peaceful orchard country. The glowing summer sunlight and the serene faces of the country people going about their work amid the olive groves give it the look of a latter-day Arcadia such as Poussin might have painted. Algajola, on the coast road, is today a peaceful little town despite its grim and lowering fortress. Lumio, with its Tuscan climate, seems totally to have escaped the ravages of time.

At Nebbio there is a fine old Romanesque cathedral, while up in the mountains behind Saint-Florent stands one of Corsica's most extraordinary buildings, the 12th-century **church of Saint-Michel at Murato**. With its remarkable polychrome stone walls displaying a strange patchwork of colours, it has all the mystery and poetry of a church in a medieval Siennese painting.

The church of Saint-Michel at Murato.

Many centuries separate the warriors who lie buried beneath the megalithic dolmens in the Tizzano valley from the victims of the vendettas described in the 19th century by Prosper Mérimée, but they are nevertheless linked by Corsica's strife-ridden history.

Corsica, which the Greeks referred to affectionately as "the most beautiful", has always had a unique destiny. Its geographical position and the poverty and injustice that have been recurrent factors in its tumultuous history have combined to shape a race of taciturn, violent men who slowly became conscious of their originality and the uniqueness of their way of life. The outside world still knows little of them, usually contenting itself with the clichés the peoples of the north regularly use to describe those of the Mediterranean world. It is almost as if the northern world suffers from an inferiority complex towards the south which it has so often conquered and subdued.

Many things have been said and written about the Corsicans. They have often been characterized as indomitable, proud, and sometimes wild. Corsican folklore has undoubtedly furnished the visitor from the mainland (known traditionally as the *pinzutu,* the man with the pointed hat) with a rich store of material for his imagination to work on. One visitor whose picture of the Corsicans comes close to the truth is Prosper Mérimée, whose stories *Colomba* and *Mateo Falcone* are set on the island. *Mateo Falcone* is the story of a father who kills his son because he has betrayed the family honour, while in *Colomba* the eponymous heroine is a young Corsican girl who urges her unwilling brother to commit murder to avenge their dead father. Colomba was not just the figment of an artist's imagination; she existed as Mérimée described her, and **the old women of Corsica** today would not have to dig too deeply into their memories to come up with similar stories. One can easily imagine them singing the *voceri,* the gloomy funeral dirges that extoll the glory and the bitterness of the vendetta, that violent, bloody institution of honour and death. Many instances of Corsican pride and stubbornness could be cited, old and new. It seems that the ancient Romans would never accept slaves from Corsica because they could get no work out of them. And who can forget that during the Second World War the Corsicans organized a redoubtable resistance and that in 1943 the island was the first part of metropolitan France to free itself from the German yoke? Mainland Frenchmen sometimes joke about the Corsican passion for honour and justice, but in doing so they misunderstand the people and their history. The Corsican character has been shaped in the course of centuries, by a sometimes-bitter experience, by hardship and the need to eke out an existence from inhospitable terrain. A striking resemblance has been forged between the harsh and beautiful island and its people.

But in a rapidly-changing world Corsica too is changing. Each year the tourists arrive in greater numbers. For them Corsica means many things: the beauty of isolated villages like **Sari d'Orcino** high in the mountains above Ajaccio, accessible only by difficult roads; memories of **Napoleon** — and there is a multitude of these all over the island; **Cap Corse** and the cliffs of **Nonza** whose citadel was defended by one man against an invading French force of 1,200 in 1768; a **shepherd** tending his flock; the lighthouse of **the Iles Sanguinaires**. These three rust-red islands, constantly battered by the waves, take on fantastic hues of scarlet or violet in the setting sun.

Old woman of Corsica.

Nonza.

Sari d'Orcino.

The statue of Napoleon at Ajaccio, by Seurre.

Corsican shepherd.

The Pointe de la Parata and the Iles Sanguinaires.

The Pyrenees and Roussillon

Between the Pyrenees and the Mediterranean lies the sun-baked ancient land of Languedoc, its name a reminder of the old southern French word "oc" meaning "yes". (The modern French "oui" comes from the old northern French word for yes—"oïl".)

Perpignan: the procession of the Sanch.

Listen to the crystal-clear welcoming notes of the old Catalan folk-songs. Hear the warm voices of the people, redolent of the sun-drenched earth, as their words pour out in a torrent of eloquence. Languedoc is a riot of exuberant colours, orchards and vineyards heavy with grapes, contrasting with the brown austerity of sun-baked rock and the aridity of windswept summits. Delicate Romanesque arches and simple villages wait to be admired in the sunshine, before you move on into the chill shadows cast by fortress-citadels and proud fortified churches. You will meet tough, secretive men given to outbursts of passion and gloomy silences pierced by sudden flashes of gaiety. Roussillon and the Pyrenees are the gateway to a France of sharp contrasts, alternately drenched with sun and overcast with shade, where traces of the long and intensely civilizing Arab influence can still be detected and the flavour of the Spanish presence is reflected in many aspects of life.

If you want your first encounter with this region to be one of pure enjoyment, then go to the Côte Vermeille, where the Pyrenees plunge into the sea. **Perpignan**, whose colours are those of an African town, was once the capital of a sea-borne empire which extended from Montpellier to the Balearic islands. From that period it has preserved fine buildings such as the 12th-century palace of the kings of Majorca, the Castillet, the rose-brick château which once guarded the city, and a 14th-century trade market known as the "Loge de Mer". On Good Friday there is a procession of penitents wearing hoods, known as the **procession of the Sanch**, which has many similarities with the Holy Week processions in Seville.

From Perpignan move on to **Collioure**, dominated by green and red hills. The sun is orange, the sky and the sea are violet. At the beginning of the century this town captivated young painters like Henri Matisse, André Derain, Raoul Dufy and Juan Gris.

Artists and anchovy fishermen rub shoulders in the "Maura", an old quarter of Collioure which has a lot in common with a North African casbah. In 1945 this charming port was awarded the simple but superb title of "city of painters".

Nearby is the little town of Banyuls, the ancient Roman settlement of Balnea, with its pretty bay sharply etched out of schist rock. An added attraction is the natural sweet wine produced nearby, to which Banyuls has given its name.

Above Banyuls the old road linking France and Spain runs across the Pyrenees, which in parts of Roussillon rise to 2,000 metres above sea level. The earth is arid in these mountain fastnesses and the sun beats down fiercely. But occasionally a lovely haven of fertility appears in the parched landscape: a flower garden known locally as a "horta", watered by a fast-flowing mountain torrent which sometimes overflows its banks and destroys its own work.

This part of France has some delightfully unpretentious churches of monastic simplicity, which modestly but admirably exemplify the unique Catalan variant of Romanesque architecture. Arles-sur-Tech, whose abbey church dates from 778, has many colourful folk traditions which reveal a strong Spanish influence. The township of Elne possesses one of the most beautiful medieval cloisters in Europe; it dates from the 11th century. The museum at Céret houses a number of Cubist works—several Cubist painters lived and worked in the town. The cellist Pablo Casals lived for many years in the orchard-encircled town of Prades, organizing its annual music festival. Three superb abbeys in the region repay a visit: Saint-Michel-de-Cuxa (whose cloister has unfortunately been transported to New York); Saint-Martin-du-Canigou; and Serrabone. Even higher, the Cerdagne basin and the upper valley of the Aude are beautiful, wild and still unspoilt.

In the early Middle Ages, these mountains bristling with fortresses protected Foix and Toulouse, the Aveyron and the Albigeois plateau against Saracen invasions. But in fact the most terrible invasion of all came from the north. In the 13th century invading barons from the Ile de France and Flanders devastated rich and highly civilized Occitania as part of the crusade against the Albigensian heretics and brought the province beneath the yoke of the Capetian kings. The fortress-churches built during the Inquisition, when the Church's military victory was assured after a century of war, show that the Church was still not sure of its spiritual victory over the stubborn Occitans. The bright-red, **cathedral-fortress of Albi** has obviously known violence and threats of destruction. It is a church built to honour a God of suspicion and anger.

Its walls are the walls of a castle, pierced by inaccessible

Albi: the painted ceiling of the cathedral.   Albi: the cathedral of Sainte-Cécile.

windows, and the belfry is a 78-metre-high keep. The bishop's palace is a fortified emplacement with keeps protected by curtain walls. But behind the stark walls of the cathedral is all the gilded luxury which shocked the austere Albigensians: a **superb painted ceiling** showing the Last Judgment (see p. 102); statues marked with Burgundian influence, displaying a violent, tortured expressionism. For the men who built this cathedral, God was clearly a threatening Inquisitor, walled in by barricades.

Albi cathedral looks more like a fortress than a church, despite an attempt by Louis d'Amboise in the late 15th century to make it look less warlike by adding a Gothic crown to the bell-tower and a "baldaquin" or flamboyant-style porch, which has been compared to "a knot of lace tied around a sword-hilt".

After a visit to Albi, military architecture tends, paradoxically, to look lighter and less aggressive. **The château of Salses**, a well-balanced brick and stone fortress set in the midst of vineyards, is today more evocative of peace than war. Standing near the coast not far from the Étang de Leucate, it was built in 1497 by Dom Sanche de Castille to bar the gateway of Roussillon to the French. Like all fortresses reputed to be impregnable it was finally captured, in 1642, though not without a hard struggle. The victorious French razed its keep to the ground, though the great military architect Vauban later restored the fort.

The old fortified town of **Carcassonne**, midway between Toulouse and the Mediterranean, dates back to the Middle Ages and was once, reputedly, the largest walled city in Europe. Today it looks like a brand-new child's toy or the setting for some cloak and dagger film, thanks to some skilful restoration work by Viollet-le-Duc at the end of the 19th century. Five hundred years after the castle was built everything—double encircling walls, port-cul-

Carcassonne.

The château of Salses.

lises, moats, loopholes and barbicans—seems to be in perfect working order.

Within its formidable double walls, the mediaeval dream takes flesh. Along the steep narrow streets lined with fine houses the craftsmen still have their workshops, just as in the Middle Ages. The church of Saint-Nazaire has survived relatively unscathed since then with its superb stained-glass windows, its Gothic choir and its pillars flanked by fine statues. In the town square an old well is still to be seen. According to local legend, a priest was once thrown into it as a punishment for his unfortunate

habit of charging for masses, but not bothering to say them: apparently his groans can still be heard.

Recent excavations have unearthed the tomb of bishop Radulph whose face still smiles a calm, Buddhic smile.

From the ramparts there is a superb view over the surrounding countryside. Each year a festival of dramatic art is held at the foot of the castle walls, taking over from the local children for whom it is normally a ready-made adventure playground. There they re-enact in their games the history of their ancient town: the sieges and skirmishes and the daring deeds of the legendary Black Prince.

There are many charming old villages to be seen in southwest France, in addition to fortresses and châteaux. One such village is Cordes, where little seems to have changed since it was built, between 1222 and 1224, by the Count of Toulouse. But most interesting of all are the region's outstanding examples of religious architecture, particularly its Romanesque churches.

Around the year 1000, long before the Albigensian crusade laid waste the countryside, there were many talented stone-masons living and working between Toulouse and Perpignan. As proof of their skill, they have left behind examples of fine vaulting, intricately carved cloisters, and numerous statues bearing strong traces of the influence of Byzantine art. Among this fine workmanship are some indisputed masterpieces.

The twin churches of Saint-André-de-Sorède and Saint-Genis-des-Fontaines, whose lintels date from 1020, are two examples of their work. These churches are among the earliest examples in Roussillon of a Romanesque art marked by the Mozarabic style from Cordoba. These masons also built the church of Rieux-Minervois, with its rounded nave and choir; the strange 12th-century "trefoiled" church at Planès, which may originally have been a mosque; and the abbey of Fontfroide, whose walls are a delightful combination of different shades of sandstone. In pure Catalan style is the priory of Monastir del Camp, thought to have been built on the orders of Charlemagne.

At **Saint-Bertrand-de-Comminges**, a beautiful old town mainly dating from medieval and Renaissance times, these skilled stone-masons built for the pilgrims travelling to Saint Jacques of Compostella a huge church with 70 carved stalls and a remarkable pink stone cloister. Finally, at Toulouse they built the magnif-

Saint-Bertrand-de-Comminges: the cloister.

icent basilica of Saint-Sernin, consecrated in 1096 by Pope Urban III. This outstanding piece of Romanesque architecture, 115 metres long and 75 metres wide at its transept, is France's biggest Romanesque church. Over the centuries, thousands of pilgrims knelt in prayer in its five aisles, supported by pillars decorated with 500 capitals. The apse is built in a mixture of brick and pale stone. The crypt contains an exceptional collection of relics, while the ambulatory has some of the oldest examples of Languedoc stone carving: seven marble low-reliefs dating from the 11th century.

As well as its Romanesque treasures, **Toulouse** also has in the church of the Dominicans (**Église des Jacobins**) one of the great masterpieces of southern Gothic art. Built in the 13th century, shortly after St. Dominic had founded at Toulouse the Order of the Preaching Friars, the church was sacked after the Revolution but saved from total destruction by being used as an army barracks. It has now been restored to its original splendour. The building, which includes the unusual feature of two parallel naves, was conceived on a grandiose scale to accommodate enormous congregations, the Friars being then engaged in the crusade against the Albigensian heresy. It exemplifies new methods of architecture and a heavier style, reflecting the influence of master masons from northern France who came south in the wake of the conquering forces. Its walls are of brick, like its vaulting and the seven magnificent columns which support the vault ribs of the nave on either side. The last and most famous pillar is the "palm-tree", so named because it supports alone all the vaults of the apse, whose 22 ribs splay out all round like palm branches. Among the other outstanding features of the church of the Dominicans are its flying buttresses and its pulpit.

Toulouse: the Église des Jacobins.

The château of Puilaurens.

But the only way to really understand the life of the far southwest of France is to leave Toulouse and Carcassonne behind and set off at random through the country villages, stopping now and then to contemplate the towering fortresses which scatter the landscape. They cling like eyries high up on the Fenouillèdes and the Corbières, the proud, arid flanks of the Pyrenean foothills. You should visit **Puilaurens**, **Peyrepertuse**, Quéribus and Montségur, where the Albigensians made their desperate last stand in 1244. Unlike **the château of Foix**, rebuilt at the end of the Middle Ages, nothing survives of them today but ruins, but they still bear eloquent witness to Occitania's tumultuous past.

The château of Foix.

The château of Peyrepertuse.

At the time of the Saracen invasion they played a valiant defensive role. But above all they were silent spectators of the final act of a tragedy which took a century to unfold: the destruction of Occitanian culture.

Occitania is a modern name, invented relatively recently. In the 11th and 12th centuries the free towns such as Toulouse and the counties which were virtually independent of the French crown were still considered part of Provence. At this period northern Europe was in a rough, almost barbaric state, except where the abbeys exerted their civilizing influence, whilst southern France was still profoundly influenced by the Greek and Roman cultures. A sixty-year-long Arab occupation followed by close trading links with the Islamic world had created a unique intellectual climate. After the Saracen conquest a civilization developed which transformed Toulouse, Montpellier, Albi, Foix and Carcassonne into dazzling intellectual centres. Their opulence and display became a byword among travellers. Every lord was a patron of the arts, every château had its floral displays and poetry competitions. In carefully-polished verses the troubadours hymned a revolutionary form of love: courtly love. It was, as one of them was later to write, the "happy time of valiant men who knew how to lay siege to estates, but also how to live for weeks on end in a court of happy people".

The Atlantic Coast

Salies-de-Béarn.

The old provinces and regions that make up France's south-west littoral—the Basque country, the Landes, the Aunis and the Vendée—differ in many respects but they all have one important thing in common: they are washed by the breakers of the Atlantic and access to the ocean has always influenced their history and development. From the Spanish border to Brittany, every little seaport has the same characteristic smell: a heady mixture of ozone, seaweed and spices; and the same atmosphere of infinite possibilities and escape as the boats set out to sea.

Follow the Pyrenees northwards, cross the Bigorre mountains and you will come to Lourdes, visited by thousands of pilgrims every year, and the ancient frontier province of Béarn, where you can fish for salmon in rushing mountain torrents or take the waters in pretty spa towns like **Salies-de-Béarn**, west of Pau. In places like this, with its picturesque old half-timbered houses, the memory of the genial Henri IV, native of the Béarn and king of Navarre before he became king of France, still lives on.

Between the Béarn and the Atlantic is the homeland of Europe's most mysterious people, the Basques. They have a reputation for being ready for anything and often live up to it. Many of them are farmers or shepherds, indissolubly wedded to their cool green mountains. You will come across them by chance in the village streets of Basse Navarre, their berets worn jauntily sideways over one ear. They are silent men, used to the solitude of the mountains, with only their animals for company. Even in **the picturesque markets** where

Hendaye bay.

they buy and sell their livestock, they seem to get by with as few words as possible. Don't underestimate them. The Basques are used to the ways of the world; few things can ruffle their imperturbability.

No one knows where the Basques came from, nor where their language originated, although some Basque words have slight similarities with Japanese and with the form of Hebrew spoken in ancient Sumer.

The Basques have always been adventurous and proficient sailors. Hundreds of years ago they hunted whales, and they were almost certainly the first people from the "Old World" to discover Newfoundland. Many of them have emigrated to South America, but the Basque homeland in Europe remains the seven provinces, four Spanish and three French (Basse-Navarre, Labourd and Soule) crowded together in that corner of the Pyrenees where France, Spain and the Atlantic meet.

The Basques have always shown a cool disregard for customs officers and frontier police, preferring to cross the border by the remote mountain

Saint-Jean-de-Luz: the church of Saint-Jean-Baptiste.

paths. The Basque smuggler is now a stock figure, like the Corsican bandit.

For centuries the Basques lived from pastoral farming, fishing and making the famous rope-soled sandals known as *espadrilles*. Since the 19th century, however, tourists have been coming to this part of France, attracted by its healthy, bracing climate, its fine beaches, picturesque fishing ports and the fascinating wealth of ancient Basque traditions. Biarritz, beautifully situated on the Gulf of Gascony, was launched during the Second Empire by the Empress Eugénie and was France's smartest and most famous seaside resort until the Second World War. It is still one of the most luxurious. Almost as famous is **Hendaye** with its vast beach, bracing sea air and dazzling sunshine. Like Biarritz it was once a fishing port. **Saint-Jean-de-Luz** with its long beach looking out onto a quiet bay is both a seaside resort and a picturesque fishing port, mainly concentrating on tunny fishing. **The church of Saint-Jean-Baptiste**, where Louis XIV's marriage to Maria Theresa of Spain was celebrated, is an exuberant profusion of statues, colonnades, balusters and painted panelling, not unlike the churches built by the conquistadors in South America.

To get a complete picture of the Basque country, however, you must not confine your visit to famous resorts like Biarritz, Hendaye and Saint-Jean-de-Luz. Ciboure, across the Nivelle river from Saint-Jean-de-Luz, is a "must", along with nearby Socoa and Guéthary, which offers a superb view of the Rhune mountain. Don't miss Bidart, known as the "Basque village by the sea", nor inland towns such as Cambo-les-Bains

The great sand dune at Pilat.

and Iraty. Iraty lies at the foot of the citadel which guarded the Roncevaux pass, where in 778 the Basques ambushed Charlemagne's troops and killed his nephew Roland—the incident which originated the famous *Song of Roland*.

North of the Basque country are the Landes. Dunes interspersed with ponds and forests ripple away to the horizon from the Adour river in the south as far as the Pointe de Grave at the mouth of the Gironde.

Ever since the 18th century, pines as well as cork-oak trees have grown along this part of the French coast. Then in the 19th century it was realized that they seemed to stop the sand dunes from spreading inland. During the Second Empire the pine plantations were extended from the coast to the marshes in the interior, which began to be drained during the construction of the Bordeaux-Bayonne railway. Until then the "landes" had been poor marshy ground where the people used tall stilts to get about.

The main tourist centre is Arcachon, situated on a sheltered bay celebrated for its **oyster-beds**. It is a favourite summer holiday resort for the people of nearby Bordeaux. At nearby **Pilat-Plage** luxurious villas are scattered around a 110-metre-high **sand dune—the highest in Europe**. In the forest near Arcachon a new winter resort has been built. It specializes in thermal treatment and has a remarkable Moorish-style casino.

Fifty kilometres to the east is Bordeaux, the proud city which is capital of Aquitaine and southwest France. In the surrounding countryside there are more than 1,500 châteaux surrounded by moats and looking out over the famous vineyards to which they have given their names: Château-Larose, Château-Lafite, Château-Latour, Château-Margaux, Saint-Estèphe and **Saint-Emilion**, where the initiation ceremony is held for the ancient brotherhood known as **the Confrérie des Jurats**. For three centuries after the marriage of Eleanor of Aquitaine to Henry Plantagenet in 1152 Aquitaine was an English possession and by the time of the 100 Years War it was already exporting its wines across the Channel. This link forged by the wine-trade strongly influenced the development of **Bordeaux**, whose **Grand Theatre** was the model for the Paris Opéra building, and it is still distinctly British in style and atmosphere.

The "Confrérie des Jurats" at Saint-Emilion.

Bordeaux: the Grand Theatre.

Oyster-beds in the bay of Arcachon.

Even when ruled by the English (between 1154 and 1453) and later (in the 16th century) when Montaigne was its mayor, Bordeaux was noted for its Roman, Merovingian, Romanesque and Gothic monuments. But it was not until the 18th century that it became one of France's most beautiful cities, through the work of two outstanding architects, Victor Louis who designed the Grand Theatre and Jacques Gabriel. They built the Allées de Tourny, the Cours du Chapeau-Rouge and the Cours d'Albert, streets lined with elegant buildings, as well as the sumptuous mansions on the *quais*—the Palais de Rohan (once the archiepiscopal palace and now the Hôtel de Ville) the Hôtel de Richelieu and the Hôtel de la Marine. They also designed the Bourse. The transformation of Bordeaux was completed around 1828 with the public gardens and the Place des Quinconces, forming an impressive promenade in the city centre.

Still busy, dynamic and rich, Bordeaux has continued to expand since the Second World War. Each year the city organizes a music festival (known as the *Mai musical* of Bordeaux) and an arts festival (Sigma), and through its links with Africa and South America is one of the major centres of French cultural activity.

On the northern side of the Gironde estuary begins the Saintonge, with its "Coast of Beauty": 70 kilometres of pine- and oak-covered littoral where a number of pretty

The port of La Cotinière, Ile d'Oléron.

The ramparts of Brouage.

resets enjoy a mild, almost Mediterranean climate. One of them, Royan, was entirely rebuilt after being destroyed by bombing in 1945 and offers an example of good modern town planning. The Coast of Beauty also has a number of small beaches, some—such as Saint-Palais-sur-Mer—beaten by the violent breakers of the Atlantic, others sheltered and surrounded by forest. Adjoining the Coast of Beauty in the north is the "Coast of Light" with its two popular offshore islands, the Ile de Ré with its long sandy beaches and **the Ile d'Oléron**, the biggest island off the French coast. The two main holiday centres in the Ile d'Oléron are Saint-Trojan-les-Bains and the pleasant little port of **La Cotinière**. Le Château d'Oléron, the chief port, facing the mainland, is surrounded by 17th-century fortifications.

La Rochelle, with the harbour of La Pallice nearby, is a lively town with fine arcaded streets. The three famous towers of St. Nicholas, la Chaîne and la Lanterne survive from the late medieval fortified port as reminders of La Rochelle's powerful and prosperous days. There is plenty of Simenonesque atmosphere around the port, and it comes as no surprise to learn that Simenon lived nearby for several years during the Second World War. One of his most powerful novels, *Les Fantômes du Chapelier* (translated as *The Hatter's Ghosts*) is set in the town. During the Reformation La Rochelle became an important centre of French Protestantism and suffered several sieges. In 1628, the subject of a famous attack by Richelieu's forces, the city, led by its mayor Jean Guitton, held out until all its ammunition and food supplies were exhausted. Then its fortifications were dismantled.

La Rochelle: the harbour.

South of La Rochelle a deserted town surrounded by ramparts emerges from the marshland and meadows. This is **Brouage**, at first sight so unreal it might be a mirage. In the Middle Ages it was the most important salt market in Europe and one of France's most prosperous ports. In 1640 Richelieu stationed 6,000 troops there. Then the port sanded up, the climate became unhealthy and the town was abandoned. Today it has become a curious museum-town, with its 17th-century walls, its food stores, its arsenal, its oven for making cannon balls, its forge, powder magazine, church and houses.

Ile d'Yeu: Port-Joinville.

Leave the Saintonge and the Aunis behind and prepare to explore the mysterious **marshes of Poitou** between Niort, Fontenay-le-Comte, Luçon and Les Sables-d'Olonne. You will find yourself in a world of drooping willows and avenues of water, a world of absolute silence. The marshes were partly drained in the 17th century by Dutch engineers, but enough of them were left to form today's waterways, along which you can sail through tunnels of foliage in special flat-bottomed boats known as *plates*. On an island in the marshes the remains of St. Peter's abbey can still be seen. Built between the 11th and 15th centuries, it once provided Rabelais with a refuge. In the last century the marshes were inhabited only by recluses, known as *huttiers*—hut-dwellers. Then, as new land was drained, a strange custom evolved for claiming it. A man who built a hut sufficiently solid to support a roof, lit a fire in it and stayed there overnight, became the undisputed owner of the plot.

But the Atlantic coast of France has many other enchanting spots. On the edge of the Poitou marshes begins the *bocage* of the Vendée. (The *bocage* country consists of a patchwork of small, irregular, hedge-enclosed fields, with numerous trees.) The countryside around La Roche-sur-Yon, between Challans and Bressuire, is typical, with its sunken roads, its châteaux and manors which, in the last decade of the 18th century, during the revolt of the Vendéc against the fledgling French Republic, sheltered many a rebel leader. But the *bocage* also includes Mount Mercure with its magnificent panoramic view, and the ruins of the château of Tiffauges, home of the child-slaughterer Gilles de Rais, comrade-in-arms of Joan of Arc. On the eastern edge of the *bocage* south-west of Poitiers is Lusignan, surrounded by fortresses which, so legend has it, were built in a single night by the fairy Melusine afters she emerged from the forest of Vouvant.

Beyond the cornfields and the valleys covered with rich pastureland is a coastline similar in many ways to that of Brittany: rocky with overhanging ledges and magnificent sandy beaches, its bays land-locked with cliffs that are almost Provençal, so bright is the colour of the sea and the rock, so luminous the air.

The islands of Noirmoutier and Yeu, off the coast of the Vendée, have such a mild climate that one might well be in the Canaries or Madeira. Noirmoutier, which can be reached on foot from the mainland at low tide by crossing the Gois causeway, has excellent beaches and a pretty wood of oak trees, La Chaise.

Palms, fig trees and eucalyptus grow on the Ile d'Yeu. On the south of the island is an attractive stretch of rugged coastline, the "côte sauvage", with plenty of rocks for sun-worshippers to stretch out on. The fishing port of **Port-Joinville** is a peaceful harbour where, on summer evenings people stand gossiping on the quayside waiting for the fishing boats to return.

Even at the height of summer, the Vendée is still relatively calm and empty. This is not the least attraction of this discreet and unsung coast, which sometimes seems keener to protect its treasures than to flaunt them.

The marshes of Poitou

The Limousin and the Périgord

Nohant.

The road from the Ile-de-France to France's south-west crosses a serene countryside of thick woods and noble rivers, rich in history and graceful old buildings. It crosses the Sologne, hunting country, before swerving off into Poitou, skirting the Auvergne and plunging deep into the Périgord.

The Sologne first of all. This land of woods, ponds, bulrushes, oaks and silver birches, gorse and farmland, is a hunter's paradise. It was here, in the quiet **village of Nohant**, on the banks of the river Indre, that George Sand lived and set some of her most famous novels. Here she entertained Chopin, Balzac and Delacroix.

The Sologne is part of Berry, and in Berry we are already in château country: the keep of Sancerre on a splendid site not far from the Loire; Mehun-sur-Yèvre, once the favourite residence of the dukes of Berry, now in ruins, although we can guess at its original appearance from the miniatures of the *Très Riches Heures* (see page 155); Valençay, designed by Philibert Delorme, was once owned by Talleyrand.

Near Châteauroux, at Déols, are the remains of a Benedictine abbey whose Gallo-Roman crypt has survived, although of the church itself only the belfry is left.

France consists essentially of a north and a south. **Poitiers**, where the advance of Islam into Europe was halted centuries ago, stands right on the border. Its **cathedral of Notre-Dame-la-Grande** with its magnificent carved façade is one of the most beautiful examples of Romanesque art in south-west France.

Poitiers: the nave c
Notre-Dame-la-Grande cathedra

Cahors: the Pont Valentré.

Argenton-sur-Creuse.

with its seven aisles and nine cupolas.

Poitiers has witnessed many great events in French history. Not far away, at Vouillé, is the battlefield where the Visigoths of Alaric II fought the Franks of Clovis in 507 A.D. Alaric was killed and Poitou fell under Frankish dominion. It was near Poitiers in 732 that Charles Martel halted the Saracen invasion led by Abd al-Rahman and saved Christian civilization in Europe.

The battle of Poitiers, in September 1356, was the second of the three great English victories of the Hundred Years War. The battle saw the defeat and capture of the French king John II the Good by a 7,000-strong Anglo-Gascon army led by the Black Prince. Four years later the Treaty of Brétigny ceded Poitou to Edward III of England and the province remained in English hands until it was won back for the French crown by the great warrior Du Guesclin. It was at Poitiers that Charles VII was proclaimed king of France in 1422 and in 1429 Joan of Arc was interrogated there in the ducal palace, today occupied by the law courts.

Not far from Poitiers are the pretty valleys of the Vienne and its tributaries, the Creuse and the Gartempe, a paradise for picnickers and anglers. The old town of Chauvigny, on the

But Poitiers has a number of other architectural masterpieces. The brick baptistery of St. John, just south of the cathedral, dates from the 4th century and is the oldest building of Christian Gaul. In the crypt of the church of St. Radegunda (d. 587) is a tomb which once contained the body of the saint, wife of the Frankish king Clotaire I and patron saint of Poitiers. The church of Saint-Hilaire-le-Grand, in the south-west of the city, is unlike any other in France, pilgrim route to Saint Jacques of Compostella, has no less than five châteaux, built between the 12th and 15th centuries. Châtellerault, on the Vienne, has a number of fine 16th- and 17th-century houses.

Many of the villages in the region have fine Romanesque churches once connected with the great abbey of Fontevrault, where there are eight Plantagenet royal tombs, including those of Henry II and his wife Eleanor and Richard I. At Montmorillon on the Gartempe is a curious 12th-century octagonal church, which may once have been a sepulcral chapel, and at Saint-Savin there is a Benedictine abbey church as famous and as beautiful as the basilica of Vézelay. It contains the richest group of Romanesque murals in the world.

The tower-porch is embellished with paintings of the Apocalypse, while the vaulting in the nave is decorated with scenes from Genesis and Exodus. The story of Christ's Passion is depicted on the walls of the organ-loft, in the crypt the martyrdom of St. Savin and St. Cyprian. The beauty of the frescoes is matched by that of the church itself.

One of the prettiest villages in the Creuse valley is **Argenton-sur-Creuse**, much favoured by anglers. It has a ruined château and picturesque houses on each bank of the river.

Aubusson, on the road from Clermont-Ferrand to Limoges, is another pretty old town that has a distinguished place in French history. If local legend is to be believed, tapestries were already being woven there at the time of Charles Martel and the Saracen invasion. Whether or not this is true, the fact remains that Aubusson tapestries first became widely famous and admired in the 15th century, when the Counts of the Marche imported Flemish weavers to work in the town. The tapestry workshops disappeared during the Revolution, but were revived during the Second

Empire when their major activity was the reproduction of classic tapestries such as the series of scenes from La Fontaine's *Fables* designed by the 18th-century animal painter Oudry.

When the art of tapestry seemed to be dying out, during the Second World War, it found a devotee in the French painter Jean Lurçat, who

revived the ancient art. His example was followed by other artists and ever since then the Aubusson workshops have never looked back.

Further south, in the Lot département, is the old town of **Cahors**, whose **Valentré bridge** spanning the river Lot is one of the best-preserved fortified bridges in France.

Aubusson: a tapestry workshop.

125

The Dordogne valley.

Collonges-la-Rouge

The bridge was built by the bishops of Cahors during the Hundred Years War and itself took 100 years to complete. With its six great Gothic arches and three noble square towers, it has become the symbol of the town. But it should not be allowed to overshadow Cahors' other important buildings, chief among which is the cathedral of St. Etienne. Built in 1119 and partially rebuilt between 1285 and 1500, it has a magnificent Romanesque portal and was the first cathedral in France to have cupolas.

Other sights in Cahors include the archdeaconry of St. John, the Hôtel de Roaldès and the old houses in the Badernes quarter which lean out over narrow streets which have scarcely changed in centuries. They evoke the atmosphere of the golden age of Cahors in the 13th century when it became well known as a financial centre and later when a university was founded there by Jacques Duèze, a native of the town who is better known as John XXII, the great Avignon pope.

127

On the borders of the Limousin are the Quercy and the Périgord, the valleys of the Lot, **the Dordogne**, the Célé and the Vézère. Few do not succumb to the charm and beauty of this rich, expansive part of France.

On the banks of the Vézère near to **Collonges-la-Rouge**, with its sandstone houses festooned with green vines, are the sites of a number of prehistoric settlements. They are beautiful, rugged and austere. The old walled town of Uzerches rises between two curves of the river, its houses clinging to the side of a steep hill. At Treignac the people will show you the Druids' Stone and the Madwomen's Rock, part of a mythology which is as old as the hills.

As it flows down from the heights of the Auvergne and enters the Périgord, the Dordogne gradually becomes less turbulent and flows along as if it had all the time in the world. Its broad meandering progress has shaped the geography of the river basin. The landscape loses much of its austerity and becomes more graceful and languid as the Dordogne flows through a fertile, well-tended land of manor-houses, châteaux and tiny ancient villages where many forms of art have flourished.

The scenery of the Dordogne has sometimes been compared with that of Greece. The valley of Tempé, where Fénelon set his *Télémaque*, a treatise written for the education of the duke of Burgundy in which the adventures of Telemachus in search of Ulysses are told in the form of a political novel, is based on the valley of the Dordogne. Fénelon was born in Perigord and wrote *Télémaque* at **the abbey of Carennac**, whose tympanum is a masterpiece of Romanesque sculpture.

One might even imagine that Fénelon acquired the nobility and loftiness of intellect which made him a suitable teacher for a prince through contemplating the spacious countryside around the château of Fénelon, his birthplace.

There are at least a dozen fine manor-houses in the valley of the Dordogne, such as Montfort, Castelnaud and Les Milandes, where Josephine Baker set up her community of children from all over the world. **Beynac**, built between the 13th and 16th century, is another fine old house. Standing on a site overlooking the valley, it has elegant corbelled towers and a collection of 15th- and 16th-century naive paintings. Beynac still has the medieval atmosphere of a château built to be celebrated by a troubadour from the age when poets had time to sing of the joys of life, women and courtly love.

Downstream, the Protestant town of Bergerac specializes in tobacco-growing. The nearby vineyards of Monbazillac produce a delicious white wine. Right on the edge of the Bordelais country is the fortified farm which belonged to Michel de Montaigne, the 16th-century author of the *Essays*.

The abbey of Carennac.

Beynac.

In the heart of the Dordogne and summing up all its history is the town of Périgueux. Originally the settlement of a Gaulish tribe, it later became a Roman town, Vesunna. The remains of the Gallo-Roman walls and the amphitheatre can still be seen. Its cathedral of Saint-Front, built in the 12th century, has the shape of a Greek cross, with five lofty domes. It was restored in the 19th century by Paul Abadie, architect of the Sacré-Cœur in Paris, who created its somewhat Byzantine appearance.

Until 1699, the 12th-century church of Saint-Etienne was Périgueux's cathedral. This Romanesque structure has a superb gilded altarpiece dating from the 17th century. The House of the Consuls, in the quarter on the bank of the Isle river, has a fine machicolated gallery surmounted by high Renaissance dormer windows. And of course Périgueux is renowned for its cooking, its truffles and its *foie gras*.

Another place where you can enjoy the same exquisite and refined cooking based on rare mushrooms and delicious but light *foie gras* is the highly civilized town of **Sarlat**. Except for one modern road, the Traverse, Sarlat is a jumbled labyrinth of streets lined with houses from many periods, their facades a lovely shade of light ochre. Roofs of volcanic stone or flat tile add to the charm. Explore the winding streets of the old town. You will find a wonderfully-preserved record of French urban architecture from the 14th to the 17th century, from the Gothic windows of the Hôtel Plamon to the splendid Renaissance **hôtel La Boétie**, the house where the 16th-century writer and humanist Étienne de La Boétie was born.

Finally, the Dordogne is rich in remains of prehistoric man. The caves of **Lascaux** in the valley of the Vézère near Montignac which were discovered by chance in 1940 in par-

Sarlat: the house of La Boétie.

Cave paintings of Lascaux.

ticular provide remarkable wall paintings and other evidence of prehistoric cultures.

Lascaux, which has had to be closed to visitors to protect the paintings from damage from bacteria, is the most beautiful link with prehistoric times in the world. The paintings are richer and more graceful than anywhere else, their colours brighter, their narrative thread more powerful.

The art of Lascaux had a definite function. The leaping horses, cows and bulls may well have been intended to influence magically the success of the hunting expeditions upon which the survival of the community depended. Hundreds of vigorous and lifelike animal figures are depicted on the walls of Lascaux. They are the work of artists who knew the animals around them intimately and displayed an extraordinary skill in painting, contrasting black, brown, red and yellow paints to enhance the realism of their work. The technical ability revealed at Lascaux shows prehistoric man to have been a highly evolved human being.

Although no god is depicted at Lascaux, the paintings are suffused with a sense of the divine mystery and one can readily understand why these caves should have been described as "underground cathedrals".

During the Ice Age, the Périgord may have been the centre of an empire which stretched across the Pyrenees into Spain. Lascaux and the Altamira caves in Spain illustrate similar themes and express a similar faith.

 Brittany

Between the English Channel and the Atlantic a peninsula juts aggressively forward into the wild waters and howling winds of the open sea like a ship, its stern firmly anchored to the French mainland. This vessel moored on Europe's far west is Brittany, a mosaic of many different provinces, each with its own distinctive features. But one thing unites them all: the sea, whose tidal rhythms dominate and govern their lives. And just as life on board ship is always a little different from life ashore, so maritime Brittany retains its uniqueness in an age of creeping uniformity.

In the past Brittany was composed of nine dioceses. Today it is divided administratively into five Départements. But neither of these descriptions reveals the essential fact: that there are two Brittanies.

East of a linguistic frontier which stretches from the Channel to the Atlantic are the regions around Nantes, Saint-Brieuc, Saint-Malo, Rennes and Dol where French has always been spoken. This is Upper Brittany, also known as the *pays Gallo*. West of the line are the four dioceses of Saint-Pol-de-Léon, Tréguier, Vannes and Cornouaille which constitute Lower Brittany or *Breiz Izel*. Here, in the most colourful part of the peninsula, the Breton language is spoken and Brittany's unique and haunting spirit is most concentrated.

If you decide to make an extended trip around Brittany, following in the footsteps of the medieval pilgrims who made the "Tro Breiz", the tour of Brittany, then start with *Breiz Izel* and get to know Cornouaille, the southern part of the province known as Finistère—"land's end" or "the end of the earth". Cornouaille is a heady concentration of traditional Celtic civilization. There is an old Celtic proverb which says of Brittany: "Kant Bro, Kant giz, Kant parrez, Kant iliz"—"a hundred regions, a hundred manners, a hundred parishes, a hundred churches", and this variety is reflected in the many dialects and traditional costumes of Cornouaille, where the atmosphere changes from village to village and town to town.

The most distinctive area of all is undoubtedly the moorland country around **Pont-l'Abbé** known as the Bigouden from the name given to **the high, cylindrical headdress** worn by the women who live there. Near **Penmarc'h**, fig trees grow outdoors in gardens sheltered by low walls. Between Ile-Tudy and **Saint-Guénolé** are a dozen tiny ports where the return of **the fishing boats** at dusk is always a captivating sight.

Penmarc'h.

Fishing boats in harbour.

The bonnets of Pont-l'Abbé.

Saint-Guénolé.

133

Tronoën:
the calvary.

The Pointe du Raz and the Baie des Trépassés.

In the Bigouden country is the sanctuary of **Tronoën**, the oldest calvary in Brittany, which stands in the flat expanse of fields stretching around the Bay of Audierne. The site of the sanctuary has been sacred ever since the pre-Christian era, and it is even said that Venus was once worshipped there.

It is a massive monument of rough-hewn rock, carved with a teeming multitude of tiny figures which form a sharp contrast with the solitude of the site. Christ, the Saints, the Apostles, Pontius Pilate, Mary Magdalene and other biblical figures are depicted on the calvary in various settings: the Garden of Eden, the Mount of Olives and Limbo, between Heaven and Hell. The Virgin Mary is represented as a tender young mother.

Like all Breton calvaries, Tronoën is an enigmatic piece of work. It is, like them, not a very ancient monument. Tronoën dates from the 15th century, and many other Breton calvaries were produced during the Renaissance. They are less the products of a naive folk art than the work of professional studio-trained artists, who set out to strengthen the Christian faith in Brittany, then considered too pagan by the Church authorities. With their suggestions of savagery, their striking realism, their depiction of the closeness of death, the religious statuary of 15th- and 16th-century Brittany achieves a haunting power which has rarely been matched and at the same time expresses the spirit of a people. Perhaps the personality of Brittany was so strong, its archetypes so deeply rooted in the collective consciousness, that the sculptors could not fail to translate them into stone.

This unique blend of toughness and mysticism and a living background of Celtic traditions can still be found in Cornouaille near **the Pointe du Raz** headland and **the Baie des Trépassés**, forming the background to the many legends which formed about the treacherous sea between the coast and the Ile de Sein. Here, at "land's end", flat green fields cap jagged cliffs which plunge sheer into the violent Atlantic waves. Winter is the time to visit this savagely beautiful coast, whose measure can best be appreciated in solitude.

At the other end of the Baie des Trépassés, less visited by tourists, is the Pointe du Van, a headland covered by a thick carpet of heather and reeds. Centuries ago, druids lived in this grandiose and desolate spot. It is said that they buried the most important of their dead across the sea on the Ile de Sein, an island of many evocative names: the Isle of the Saints, the Isle of the Old, the Isle of the Seven Sleeps, the Isle of the Nine Priestesses. According to an old Breton tradition, sacred virgins lived on the island, which was also the birthplace of Myrddin, also known as Merlin the wizard.

Along the road from the Pointe du Raz to Brest are many more famous and legendary places: Crozon; the Pointe de Toulinguet; the magnificent Chèvre peninsula; the fishing port of Camaret where you can see trawlers being built; the sea caves at Morgat; Locronan, once a sail-making centre and now protected as a town of historic interest; Sainte-Anne-la-Palud, which puts on the most popular *pardon* (saint's day celebration) in Lower Brittany; and Plougas-

Belle-Ile.

The stones of Carnac.

tel, a fertile seaside garden of Eden which is famed for its fruit and vegetables.

North of Brest is the Léon country, where the coastline is gashed with "abers" or inlets which penetrate deep inland. Best-known and prettiest is Aber Wrac'h. Between Guimiliau and Saint-Thégonnec are many old châteaux, churches and calvaries. In some churchyards one can still see ossuaries where the bones of the dead were stored after their graves were exhumed to make room for later arrivals. Out at sea is the island of Ouessant, where because of the nearness of the Gulf Stream roses, fig trees and blackberries grow in abundance. On the mainland the headland of Pointe Saint-Mathieu marks the authentic end of Europe.

This land of profound secrets has been dubbed the "coast of legend" because of its strangely-shaped rocks and its imposing stone menhirs. Many of these huge megaliths were however Christianized in the Middle Ages.

In sunnier, more open Morbihan, however, they have remained just as their mysterious devotees intended them. Near **Carnac**, the countryside between Kermario and Locmariaquer is dotted with 2,600 upright stones. No one knows who put them there or why, but few fail to be struck by their cosmic grandeur. The Morbihan is a popular holiday area, with its capital, the pretty town of Vannes, and Sainte-Anne-d'Auray, home of the biggest *pardon* in all Brittany. The fishing port of Quiberon now has a vast thalassotherapy institute, while the island of **Belle-Ile**, once a beleaguered fortified outpost of the French mainland, today attracts growing numbers of holidaymakers.

The saltmarshes
of Guérande.

Upper Brittany, with a less powerful personality than Lower Brittany, still has plenty of beauty spots, attractive towns and fine monuments. It lies east of a line running roughly from the Trégorrois country (on the Channel side of the peninsula) to the Morbihan Département (on Brittany's southern, Atlantic coast).

The Atlantic port of Nantes is the biggest city in Brittany. It has an old-established ship-building industry, but first rose to great wealth and prominence through the slave trade, whose nabobs built themselves magnificent town houses there during the 17th and 18th centuries and created much of the city as it exists today. Nantes was the birthplace of Anne of Brittany (1477-1514) whose marriage with Charles VIII of France set the seal on the union of Brittany and France. Nearby are a number of famous holiday resorts such as La Baule, Le Pouliguen and Le Croisic whose beaches are always crowded with summer visitors.

In the past the salt industry played a major role in the economy of this area on the northern shore of the Loire estuary. The old walled town of **Guérande** stands in the midst of **salt-marshes**, whose geometric patterns give this flat expanse a strange resemblance to an abstract painting in gleaming pastel colours. At dawn and dusk the drifting mist and the clouds from the open sea blur the horizon with a delicious melancholy.

The same melancholy pervades the marshlands of **the Brière**, where in the past peat was dug and flocks and herds pastured. Today the marsh people, the Briérons, still cross the marshes in flat-bottomed barges known as "blains", although the Brière itself has become a 40,000-hectare nature reserve.

The villages of the Brière have great charm, with their whitewashed houses and thatched roofs. In spring they are a mass of flowers whose pro-

In the Brière.

fusion of colours are mirrored in the still, grey waters. In autumn silver grey waters reflect a silver grey sky while huntsmen wait patiently for waterfowl, ducks and snipe.

The people who live in this highly unusual part of the world were once reputed to be wild and uncivilized. The reputation was not entirely without foundation since the Brière was once largely inhabited by freed prisoners from the prison-colonies of Guyana, perhaps the only people who could manage to survive in this desolate spot.

Rennes, halfway between the English Channel and the Atlantic, is one of the most beautiful cities in France and today one of the busiest. Before the Revolution it was the seat of the Parlement of Brittany, the region's independent-spirited high court of justice, which was often a thorn in the flesh of the French monarchy. The dignified 17th-century granite building where the Parlement sat is today occupied by the law courts. The work of Salomon de Brosse, architect of the Luxembourg Palace in Paris, it is truly Breton in inspiration.

Although situated in the *pays Gallo,* Rennes is also on the threshold of *Bretagne bretonnante*—Brittany which speaks the Breton tongue. It is also near to the Brittany of

A Soviet four-master on a visit to Saint-Malo.

Combourg.

myth and legend. The knights of the Round Table once rode through the forest of Paimpont, not far away. As the forest of Brocéliande it was the setting of the legendary story of Lancelot, King Arthur, Merlin the wizard and Viviane the sorceress. The supernatural never seems far away in Brittany and the mysterious, magical atmosphere of the quest for the grail still lingers on today in Paimpont's sombre and magnificent woods.

The great Romantic writer Chateaubriand was born not far away at the splendid feudal château of **Combourg** set amid woods and moors. As a young man Chateaubriand had only to walk a few kilometres to indulge his adolescent dreams and fantasies: in one direction towards Brocéliande, in another towards the rugged Channel coast with its jagged pink granite rocks and enchanting secluded inlets. At l'Ile-Grande near the resort of Trébeurden another medieval legend is remembered. Here was the land of King Mark of Cornouaille where

Tristan and Iseult drank the magic potion which began their saga of eternal love.

The countryside of *Arcoat* (inland Brittany; coastal Brittany is known as *Armor*) stretches from Rennes to the Channel in an undulating expanse of woodland, rivers, sunken paths and moors, here speckled gold with broom and gorse, there decked with the mauve tints of heather.

Dinard, on the estuary of the Rance, was founded by an American named Coppinger and became a fashionable resort after the Empress Eugénie spent a holiday there.

West of the Rance estuary, the Bay of Saint-Brieuc stretches from Cap Fréhel to the little fishing port of Paimpol. Here we are in the region known as the Trégorrois, where sleepy ports nestle at the head of "abers" (inlets) and where Breton is widely spoken. Perros-Guirec, Trébeurden, Ploumanac'h and Trégastel all share with the offshore island of Bréhat a mild climate (which they owe to the proximity of the Gulf Stream) and spectacular scenery—pink granite cliffs tumbling chaotically down to the emerald sea.

Across the estuary from Dinard the attractive resorts of Saint-Servan and Paramé are somewhat overshadowed by their more colourful neighbour, the old pirate town of **Saint-Malo**. Tightly packed behind its massive walls, the old town still has some attractive buildings, although it had to be extensively rebuilt after being damaged in heavy fighting between German and American troops during World War II. In the past Saint-Malo had many opulent ship-builders' houses. Behind their nail-studded doors they were furnished with beds, cupboards, dressers and tables of rare exotic woods. Today most of these houses have disappeared, but enough have survived to evoke the atmosphere of the days when Saint-Malo sailors, led by their bold captain Robert Surcouf, set sail on pirate expeditions against the English, Dutch and Spaniards.

On the quays of Saint-Malo, near the jetty, white-haired old men in seamen's caps stand binoculars in hand watching the boats come and go. Although shore-bound, it is obvious that their hearts are still out at sea.

But things are changing in Brittany today. Once poor, illiterate and outside the mainstream of French life, Brittany now has a dynamic and able younger generation, determined (like the young people of Occitania) to stay in their birthplace and make it prosperous.

Saint-Malo.

The Loire Valley

The "Mille Fleurs" tapestry at the Château of Angers.

'A homespun dress fringed with gold". It would be hard to improve on this short description, penned by the great historian Michelet in the 19th century, of the land around the middle reaches of the Loire which forms the real heart of France. It was here that the French language evolved in its purest form, achieving its first great masterpiece in the late 13th-century poem the *Roman de la Rose*. Here in the 16th century was the political nerve-centre of the French kingdom. Here above all, in Touraine, Anjou and Maine, in Blois and Orléans and their surrounding areas, four centuries of French history have left an unrivalled legacy of splendid châteaux, which were once powerful fortresses and later became country estates for kings, the nobility and the rich. From Ronsard to Balzac, the Loire is also rich in literary associations.

The ancient province of Anjou in the west was the centre of a medieval empire. Its medieval and Renaissance rulers built imposing fortresses, filled them with magnificent works of art and surrounded them with parks and formal gardens. **Angers**, the capital of

The Château of Angers.

Anjou, is still recognizably the town of René the Good, 15th-century duke of Anjou and a discerning patron of the arts. His opulent living quarters stand at the foot of the great **château** built by Saint Louis. Defended by 17 towers of granite encircled by rings of schist, the château is today a showcase for one of the world's great works of art, the *Tapestry of the Apocalypse*. The tapestry, originally 170 metres long, depicts in vivid blues and reds St. John's vision of the end of the world. It was woven in the 14th century by Nicolas Bataille.

Presented by René of Anjou to Angers cathedral, the tapestry was dismembered during the Revolution and disappeared. It was rediscovered by a 19th-century bishop of Angers who found it being used as a carpet by his officials. Today 70 of the original panels have been reconstituted and hang in the château, along with the charming series of tapestries known as **the Mille Fleurs**, which delightfully depicts the civilized pleasures of château life in old Anjou.

143

When people talk about the "châteaux of the Loire", they usually refer to the châteaux along the tributaries of the Loire as well as those on the banks of the Loire itself. Some even prefer the châteaux on the tributaries to those on the parent river. Azay-le-Rideau, in the Indre valley, has many admirers. Standing on a tiny island surrounded by a moat, the present château was begun in 1518 by Gilles Berthelot, treasurer of France, and finished six years later. It was so lavish that the king checked Berthelot's books with the result that he was later dismissed in disgrace. At Loches, also in the Indre valley, is the marble tomb of Agnes Sorel, one of the most beautiful women of 15th-century France, and favourite of Charles VII. On the banks of the Cher is the château of Montrichard, and not far away **Chenonceaux** bestrides the same river, reminding the visitor that in the Middle Ages a water-mill flanked by a semi-fortified

The Château of Chenonceaux.

manor-house occupied the same spot.

These buildings were bought by the wily Thomas Bohier, minister of Charles VIII and his successors, and yet another royal treasurer who came to grief because of his extravagant expenditure and his careless way of keeping the king's accounts (see also page 156). Bohier spent most of his time travelling all over France collecting the royal taxes and left his wife, Catherine Briçonnet, the job of making the most of the old buildings. Catherine concentrated on the mill and had the fortress demolished, except for its keep. The result was one of the most feminine of France's great houses.

Chenonceaux has always been a woman's château. No less than six have been involved in its history, among them the fascinating Diane de Poitiers, mistress of Henri II. Before this, Chenonceaux had passed to the French crown after Bohier and Catherine had been accused of dipping their fingers in the royal till to build the lovely five-arched château. Henri presented Chenonceaux to Diane de Poitiers as soon as he came to the throne in 1547 and she built new arches linking it to the opposite bank of the Cher so that she could indulge her passion for hunting more easily.

When Henri died, Diane in her turn was forced to give up Chenonceaux and restore it to the king's widow, Catherine de Médicis. Catherine too fell in love with Chenonceaux and decided to transform it into the most sumptuous château in France. She imported art treasures from Italy and engaged the architect Philibert Delorme to build a two-storey gallery over Diane's bridge for banquets and celebrations. Nothing in France at that time could rival the lavish evening entertainments given at Chenonceaux. A 75-hectare park and elegant gardens for daytime festivities completed the château's splendour.

The Vienne.

Other chatelaines have ruled over Chenonceaux right up to our own times. The present one has installed stereophonic equipment in the ground floor gallery, the only one open to visitors, playing music from the time of the Medicis. Son et Lumière shows on two themes: "Festivities in the time of Queen Catherine" and "Ladies of Chenonceaux" bring back the atmosphere of old Chenonceaux and conjure up the ghosts of the beautiful women whose lives were closely linked with it.

The smooth murmuring waters of the Loire have inspired many French poets: "I still wish to bring forth a flower on the banks of the Loire suffused with my own pale colours, reflecting my name and my pain", sang the melancholy Ronsard. And it was on the banks of the river **Vienne** that Rabelais set his Utopia, the abbey of Thélème, whose motto was "Do as thou dost wish".

145

Renaissance Italy had a strong influence on the art and architecture of the châteaux of the Loire. François I made war in Italy and was overwhelmed by the artistic explosion he saw there. He and his entourage returned to France determined to employ the great Italian artists, architects and jewellers in their palaces and châteaux. Thus it came about that Leonardo da Vinci spent much time at Amboise, a great centre of artistic activity throughout the reign of François I, and probably flew his experimental model flying machine from its towers. Chaumont has a vast mosaic floor imported from Italy, and the work of Cellini can be seen at Azay-le-Rideau. Italian architects also left their mark on the gardens of some of the Loire châteaux.

This influence is perhaps at its most striking in the famous gardens of **the château of Villandry** in the Cher valley near the confluence of the Cher with the Loire. Three terraces bordered by ditches and vines are set out one above the other. In the top one are fountains and an artificial lake almost a hectare in area. Beneath it, close-cropped box hedges have been designed to depict in allegorical form four kinds of love: tender love (a heart-shaped design), tragic love (knives), fickle love (butterflies) and adulterous love (horns). On the bottom level is a vegetable garden set out in geometric designs.

It would be impossible to visit the gardens of Villandry today were it not for the remarkable restoration work carried out in the years after 1906 by the château's owner, Dr. Carvallo. In the middle of the 18th century Villandry passed into the hands of the Marquis de Castellane who made drastic changes in the original 16th-century gardens designed for François I's Secretary of State, Jean Lebreton. Wanting to keep up with fashion, the Marquis transformed these formal gardens into an English-style park with paths, copses, oaks and weeping willows. As soon as he acquired Villandry, Dr. Carvallo set about restoring it to its original appearance.

A few kilometres from Villandry is the huge Renaissance **château of Chambord**, today the property of the French state which uses it as a de luxe hunting lodge for distinguished visitors. The château grounds are surrounded by a 32-kilometre-long wall, the longest in France. Started by François I, continued by Henri II and redecorated by Louis XIV, Chambord has no less than 440 rooms. Today, unfortunately, its interior does not match up to its grandiose exterior, since the furnishings have disappeared. But Chambord has many sights ranging from the impressive to the curious: the great spiral staircase which enabled horsemen to reach the living quarters without dismounting and is constructed so that persons going up never see those who are coming down; the richly ornamented chimneys; and the proverb which

Villandry: the formal vegetable garden.

The Château of Chambord.

The hunting museum at the Château of Cheverny.

François I once engraved on glass with his diamond ring.

It was at Chambord that François I entertained his arch enemy, the emperor Charles V, with a provocative display of ostentation. On its return from the hunt the royal party was announced by fanfares played on hunting horns and preceded by 300 falcons, hunting dogs and an army of beaters. Dressed as Greek goddesses, the loveliest ladies in the realm were there to welcome the hunters.

Chambord has one slightly comic feature: the river Cosson which flows beneath it is so tiny in comparison that one thinks inevitably of the mountain that laboured and brought forth a mouse. François I was aware of the disproportion and wanted to divert the Loire. But the project was beyond his resources.

The smaller **château of Cheverny** was built by Louis XIII in 1634. Here too the pleasures of the chase take a front seat: the château today houses a hunting museum.

No two châteaux in the Loire valley are exactly alike. Each has its own character and holds its own surprises. Menars, for example, which once belonged to Madame de Pompadour, is a graceful building with a beautiful artificial lake watched over by cherubs. **Ainay-le-Vieil** conceals a charming garden behind its austere fortifications. War and pleasure... for Balzac these symbolized the essential spirit of Touraine.

Nowhere else in France has such a finely-balanced harmony been achieved between architecture and landscape. Nowhere else have man and his environment been so perfectly integrated together and so determined to remain so. When Marshal de Saxe was master of Chambord, he executed soldiers found guilty of throwing the smallest piece of rubbish in the avenues of the park. The people of the Loire valley today still have strong feelings about preserving their heritage.

This concern for fine architecture reached its apogee during the Renaissance, but it was already deeply rooted long before then. In the mid-15th century Jacques Cœur, an outstanding businessman who became powerful as Charles VII's treasurer, built himself a palace at **Bourges** that was far more elegant and luxurious than anything a non-aristocrat had ever built before. Even today its remains evoke the splendours of Gothic domestic architecture as few other buildings can. It is also full of details, such as the stone servants that keep watch on either side of the main entrance, that are highly unusual in 15th-century French architecture. In the courtyard, a low-relief sculpture of exotic trees is a reminder of Jacques Cœur's extensive travels.

Only a few hundred metres away, crowning the summit of the hill on which Bourges is built, is **the cathedral of Saint-Étienne**, one of the most beautiful Gothic cathedrals in France. It has five magnificent doorways flanked by two asymmetrical towers. The interior has five aisles and no transepts and contains, among many works of art, outstanding stained glass windows of the 12th to the 17th century. Beneath the choir is a fine 12th-century crypt and traces of a 9th-century Carolingian church.

The Château of Ainay-le-Vieil.

The nave of the cathedral of St-Étienne, Bourges.

On the edge of the Loire valley stands **Chartres**, whose cathedral of Notre-Dame many consider to be the finest example of Gothic religious architecture in the world. The poet Charles Péguy celebrated it with a lyricism it richly deserves: "a man from our country, from our fertile soil, had a spire built here which has no equal anywhere in the world. It soars upwards in a single thrust from a single foundation towards your Assumption." "The strongest stem that ever burst upward", Péguy also wrote of Chartres cathedral.

One's first glimpse of the cathedral towers rising over the corn-fields of the Beauce, "the granary of France", is an unforgettable experience. But it is equally impressive seen within the town from the banks of the river Eure, where ancient houses nestle up to the very sides of the cathedral as if in search of protection. Built in the 12th and 13th centuries during a great wave of religious enthusiasm, Notre-Dame has been damaged and partially rebuilt several times, but none of the damage inflicted on it has spoilt the purity of its lines.

Chartres cathedral is full of masterpieces. Look closely at the majestic statues on the portals; the folds of their

Chartres: Notre-Dame de la Belle Verrière.

robes are a triumph of meticulous craftsmanship. Among the hundreds of other statues is one of the Black Virgin which has drawn pilgrimages of the devout ever since the 14th century. The simpler of the towers is a masterpiece of purity. The 13th-century stained-glass windows and the Renaissance choir screen are equally memorable. One of the themes presented in the statuary is almost unique in the history of art: Adam in the mind of God, before the creation.

Chartres also has several other noted churches: the 13th-century abbey church of St. Pierre with its fine stained glass; the Romanesque church of St. André; the Renaissance church of St. Aignan.

The scenery in the Loire valley is pretty enough to merit a visit for its own sake, and one guide-book even describes a tour of "The Loire without the Châteaux". But if it would be a pity not to see the countryside, it would be perverse not to sample the fine wines of the Loire valley in the region where they are produced. Round off a visit to the châteaux by drinking to them and their history in Vouvray, Chinon, Bourgueil or Saumur.

Chartres: the royal portal on the south-west front.

The corn-fields of the Beauce and Chartres cathedral.

15

The Ile-de-France

The Ile-de-France is the name given to the fertile region, bounded more or less by the meandering course of four rivers, the Seine, the Marne, the Oise and the Aisne, which forms Paris's green belt. Every fine weekend the Parisians pour out of the capital to relax in its woods and forests and admire its architectural treasures beneath gently shifting skies unforgettably painted by the Impressionists. The Ile-de-France has always owed much to the proximity of Paris and this partly accounts for its notable architectural wealth. No other French region can boast such a flowering of great masterpieces, stretching from the Romanesque period through the Renaissance to neo-classicism. It has at least a hundred Romanesque abbeys and churches; it contains examples of all the different currents of French Gothic; and it has a remarkable number of fine châteaux set in formal gardens and built by kings, princes, courtiers, prelates, financiers and nobles whose names are inscribed in French history.

The most famous and elaborate monument of the Ile-de-France is undoubtedly **the château of Versailles**, less than 15 kilometres from Paris. Here in the 17th century the Sun King Louis XIV decided to build a palace that would be more beautiful than any other in the world. The genius of three men, the architects Louis Le Vau and Jules-Hardouin Mansart, and André Le Nôtre who designed the gardens, combined to produce an incomparable example of French Classical art. At first the architects simply made a few alterations to the small brick and stone hunting lodge maintained at Versailles by Louis XIII, and priority was given to the gardens. With their shrubberies, tree-lined avenues and alleys, rock gardens, ornamental basins, fountains and statues of classical gods such as the marble group representing Apollo being ministered to by nymphs in **the grove of the bath of Apollo**, they are in themselves a work of art on the grand scale. Today the best way to appreciate what the château and gardens of Versailles must have been like in Louis XIV's time is to attend an evening Son et Lumière show. In the dramatic atmosphere created by multi-coloured arc-lights the fountains surge to life, the marble horses pulling **Apollo's chariot** seem to dash through the foaming waters of the basin, and one can imagine the Grand Canal covered once again with gondolas and boats as during the Sun King's reign. For 40 years Versailles teemed with activity as workmen erected scaffolding, moved earth, laid foundations, cut stone and built walls. Work began under Le Vau in 1662, continued after his death under Mansart, and was finally completed in 1701.

Versailles: thc basin of Apollo.

The château of Versailles.

Versailles: the bath of Apollo.

The basilica of Saint-Denis: the tomb of Henri II.

The château of Fontainebleau: the Council Room.

Versailles as we know it today took shape gradually: the façade with its golden balustrades; the *Cour de Marbre* (just below the central part of the palace on the front which faces Paris) where birdcages were built in the corners so that "the cooing of birds should mingle with the murmuring of the waters"; the 73-metre-long *Galerie des Glaces* (the Hall of Mirrors) the great central gallery on the first floor of the château; the Great and Small Apartments of the King; the pink and white marble Grand Trianon, built as a retreat where the king could go when he wanted to get away from the stifling formality of court life. After the Sun King's death Louis XV added his own personal touches to Versailles. He preferred to live in smaller and more intimate surroundings and so he built the so-called "small apartments" in the main building and, following the current fashion for miniature châteaux, constructed the Petit Trianon.

During the Revolution Versailles was plundered and vandalized, most of its treasures being destroyed, stolen, sold or in a few cases transferred to the Louvre. For a time there were even plans to raze the château to the ground. Today a dedicated curator, Mr. Gérald Van Der Kemp, has embarked on the task of restoring Versailles. A number of patrons of the arts, notably American philanthropists, are assisting the project which aims at nothing less than the recreation of Versailles exactly as it was in its golden age.

Even nearer Paris than Versailles, tucked discreetly away in a busy industrial suburb is one of the most important monuments in French history, **the basilica of Saint-Denis**.

The basilica is dedicated to Denis, the first bishop of Paris, who was martyred in 250 and who, according to legend, was decapitated and carried his head in his hands to the spot where he wished a church to be built. A church was first built on the site in 475 at the instigation of Saint Geneviève, the patron saint of Paris. About 630 this church was altered and extended by the Merovingian King Dagobert and in 750 it was rebuilt by Pepin the Short. Sometime around 1130 a chancel, a narthex and a bell-tower were begun by abbot Suger, the most distinguished abbot of Saint-Denis, under whom the town became a great artistic and intellectual centre. These were added to the original Romanesque nave and crypt. Finally in 1231 St. Louis entrusted the rebuilding of the abbey to Pierre de Montreuil, the greatest architect of the Middle Ages (also reputed to be an alchemist) who created the Gothic masterpiece where all French kings from the Middle Ages to the Revolution were buried. Dozens of tombs have been excavated, among them that of Queen Armegonde, wife of Clotaire III, a 7th-century king of Neustria and Burgundy. Her tomb contained fine clothes and jewellery which threw much new light on Merovingian civilization. These tombs and the recumbent figures which decorate them incidentally illustrate the history of French funerary art. Among the most famous are the tomb of Louis XII and Anne of Brittany; the tomb of François I, decorated with scenes from the battle of Marignan executed in a style which has been compared to that of Paolo Uccello; and the uncompleted **tomb of Henri II** begun by Pierre Lescot and Germain Pilon.

Further north of Paris lies the charming old town of Senlis with its lovely cathedral, and Compiègne whose château was a favourite residence of Napoleon III during

the junction of the Seine and the Oise northwest of Paris, offers a glimpse of a picturesque and colourful world. Moored along the river banks is a floating village of barges, for Conflans is one of the main assembly points for barges from all over France and the Low Countries. One barge has been converted into a floating church, and on the hill which overlooks the Seine, behind the church there is a fascinating museum of barge history.

Another of France's great royal palaces can be seen at **Fontainebleau**, 60 kilometres southeast of Paris. Begun under Philippe Auguste and Saint Louis, it was originally no more than a hunting lodge. Its chief creator, in the

Conflans-Sainte-Honorine.

The wooden market at Milly-la-Forêt.

the hunting season. At Rethondes in the forest of Compiègne the armistice ending World War I was signed in 1918. Not far away is the town of Chantilly, celebrated for its park, its horse races and its château, now an important museum containing two great treasures: 40 miniatures (once part of a large book of hours, but now dismembered) by the 15th-century painter Jean Fouquet and the 14th-century Duc de Berry's book of hours, *Les Très Riches Heures*.

The town of **Conflans-Sainte-Honorine**, which stands at

16th century, was François I who made it his chief residence and employed the best architects, sculptors and painters of the period. Commissioned by Catherine de Médicis, the architect Philibert Delorme put the final touches to the château, which has seen the birth of Louis XIII, the marriage of Louis XV, and on a famous day in 1814 Napoleon's farewell to the Imperial Guard before he set off into exile. Not far away is the charming village of **Milly-la-Forêt**, with its 15th-century wooden market hall and a chapel decorated by Jean Cocteau, who lived there.

155

Another "must" for visitors to the Ile-de-France is **the château of Vaux-le-Vicomte** south-west of Paris. Versailles was modelled on it and designed by the same team: Le Vau, Le Brun and Le Nôtre. Perhaps it would not be going too far to say that Versailles owes its existence to Vaux-le-Vicomte.

The man who built Vaux-le-Vicomte was Louis XIV's wealthy finance minister, Nicolas Fouquet. He had exceptionally good taste in art but also, so it was said, possessed an unfortunate tendency to allow his own personal finances and those of the State to become confused.

In the 17th century it was the fashion for the rich and powerful to build themselves great country residences. Fouquet's plans were on the grand scale—a whole village had to be razed to make way for his château—and as a man with a flair for discovering talent, he entrusted the work to three relatively unknown designers. Le Vau was to draw up the plans for the château, Le Brun was to decorate the interior, and Le Nôtre was to design the gardens. No less than 18,000 workmen were taken on and the work began. By August 17, 1661, everything was ready and Fouquet, who seems to have known more about art than psychology, invited Louis XIV to the opening party. The lavish celebrations spilled out into the gardens. The great Lulli was chief violinist. The catering was supervised by the renowned chef Vatel. In a theatre surrounded by greenery, Molière and his troupe performed *Les Fâcheux*. It was a perfect party except for one discordant note: the king was in a bad temper. Perhaps the ostentatious luxury of his surroundings reminded him that the royal finances were far from healthy. Perhaps he was just angry that his finance minister lived in finer style than he did. Whatever the reason for his ill-humour, he lost his temper and refused to spend the night in the château. His coach was got ready and he set off for Fontainebleau. Less than three weeks later an officer named D'Artagnan (whose fictionalized exploits were later to be made famous by Alexandre Dumas) came to arrest Fouquet. There was a trial and Fouquet was imprisoned in the fortress of Pignerol in the Alps. His only defenders at that time were Madame de Sévigné, the letter-writer and La Fontaine, author of the Fables.

As for Louis XIV, he "requisitioned" Vaux-le-Vicomte's designers and ordered them to set about transforming Versailles. Some people prefer the original, Vaux-le-Vicomte, to the copy. Vaux-le-Vicomte is certainly more homogeneous, being built entirely of stone, which was unusual at that time, and it is possible that Le Vau, Le Brun and Le Nôtre felt freer there to give full rein to their imagination. Perhaps too Nicolas Fouquet had better taste than the king and had more idea of where to draw the line between beauty and ostentation.

The beautiful green gardens and murmuring waters of Vaux-le-Vicomte make it an enchanting place to visit. Looking through the château today, including its King's bedroom where the king never slept, one can understand the perplexity of La Fontaine's remark: "Everything at Vaux conspired to please the King: the music, the waters, the lamps and the stars above."

Vaux-le-Vicomte.

Rheims cathedral: the Smiling Angel.

Rheims cathedral: the interior.

In the Ile-de-France there is a major monument or historic site at every point of the compass: Saint-Denis in the north, Versailles in the west, Fontainebleau in the south, and in the east **Rheims**, where the kings of France were traditionally crowned.

The finest architectural treasure in Rheims is **the cathedral**, but it is far from being the only building of historical and architectural interest. In fact the visitor with a little time to spare might begin his tour of Rheims with a look at the church of Saint-Rémi, a former Benedictine abbey and an interesting example of Romanesque architecture that has been exposed to Gothic influence without being overwhelmed by it. The 121-metre-long nave (exactly the same length as that of Notre-Dame in Paris) is totally Romanesque in its restraint.

The cathedral, an example of Gothic at its apogee, is one of the biggest in France, being second only to Amiens in size. One of its outstanding features is its homogeneity of style, due to the fact that it was built in less than a century (between 1211 and 1300). This remarkable unity of style gives it a special beauty. A distinctive feature of church architecture in Champagne are the stained-glass windows which decorate the tympanums. Unlike the architecture, the sculptures—of which there are an estimated 3,000—that embellish the cathedral differ widely in style. This is because the cathedral was built in such haste that several workshops produced statues for it at the same time. One workshop produced the celebrated **Smiling Angel** of Rheims, another the Annunciation scene, yet another the Visitation. The cathedral's tapestries are as outstanding as its sculptures; Rheims cathedral possesses the finest tapestry collection in France after that of Angers.

Apart from these two major landmarks, Rheims has many buildings of architectural interest which miraculously survived heavy shelling in the First World War, when Rheims was in or near the front line during the battle of the Marne. (The cathedral suffered heavy damage then and was subsequently restored.) There is a fine Gallo-Roman triumphal arch, the Porte de Mars, which is only matched in France by that at Orange. A number of fine old houses dating from various periods between the Middle Ages and the 17th century are also still standing. One of them is the 15th-century Maison le Vergeur, which today houses a fascinating museum devoted to the history of the city. The prettily-named Maison des Musiciens, another historic building dating from the same period, has been dismantled and can be seen (still in its dismantled state, unfortunately) in the city's Musée Lapidaire, which contains a number of rare ancient objects such as the tomb of Jovin, a Roman general.

Rheims's Musée des Beaux-Arts has a rich and varied collection of paintings. There are 30 canvases by Corot, as well as paintings by Le Nain, Poussin, David, Daumier, Philippe de Champaigne, Pissarro and Renoir.

Rheims is worth a lengthy visit because of its churches, its museums and its long and important role in French history. But apart from these intellectual considerations there is another, more materialistic attraction in Rheims and its neighbouring countryside. This attraction is known as Champagne, France's most famous wine. Champagne owes its sparkle to the genius of a 17th-century monk named Dom Pérignon, a brilliant blender of wines. Dom Pérignon, who is also credited with being the first to use cork-bark as the stoppers of bottles, was cellarer of the Benedictine abbey of Hautvillers between Ay and **Épernay** in the heart of the vineyards which today stretch along the chalky hillsides overlooking the majestic curves of **the Marne**. Everywhere, in the vineyards and in the cellars of the Champagne houses, one can see evidence of the meticulous skill, experience and unremitting effort which maintain the quality and reputation of this world-famous wine.

The Marne at Épernay.

16

Paris

A Republican Guard.

A soldier of **the Republican Guard**, his sword drawn for the great military parade; a fireworks display; a 300-metre-high iron tower; dancing in the streets: these images symbolize Paris in all its glory, Paris festive, Paris commemorating 14 July 1789, the day when her citizens stormed the infamous Bastille prison and thought that they had put paid to tyranny and injustice forever. **The Eiffel Tower** was in fact built for the 1889 Paris Universal Exhibition as a memorial to the French Revolution. "A great part of the civilized world will pass beneath this immense triumphal arch, symbolizing the wholly peaceful victory of the human spirit", said its designer Gustave Eiffel at the inauguration ceremony, eschewing false modesty. But Eiffel was not wrong. Paris is one of the world's most visited cities and the Tower, which Eiffel wanted "to represent for all time the art of the engineer and the century of industry and science", is Paris's most visited monument. But how should one set about "visiting" Paris? At first glance it seems an easy city to appreciate and understand, as straightforward as the logic of its ordered streets. But in fact it has its secrets and guards them jealously. The visitor who wants to know Paris must learn something of its long history, which has left an imprint on every corner of the city. The Parisians and their city cannot be dissociated: the historic buildings have no meaning except as the expression of a history and a way of life. The Parisians love Paris with a fierce pride and make it a volatile city, a city of many moods. When they take to the streets in anger and attack their city's monuments,

The Eiffel Tower.

they are committing a *crime passionnel*. And when they take to the streets in a mood of happiness, no city can go wilder with joy.

The spell of Paris is no recent thing; it goes back at least 2,000 years. When the Romans first discovered the tiny settlement of Lutetia, on what is now the Ile de la Cité, they were astonished by the attachment of the barbarian boatmen to the island on which they lived. The charm still exists; it is easier to succumb to it than explain it. Many poets have written of Paris, its splendours and its miseries: François Villon in the 15th century, Victor Hugo, Gérard de Nerval, Baudelaire and Villiers de L'Isle-Adam in the 19th, Louis Aragon in our own day. They are the best guides to this fickle city.

The Seine and the prow of the Ile de la Cité (above). The Ile Saint-Louis (below).

The Place des Vosges.

The ideal way to start exploring Paris is to stroll along the *quais* on the two islands in the heart of the city, the Ile de la Cité and the Ile Saint-Louis. Such a walk is still agreeable, since traffic is restricted in some of these riverside streets. It is also a logical way of making acquaintance with Paris, since the city's history began on the Ile de la Cité and many of its most charming aspects can be found concentrated on the Ile Saint-Louis.

The Ile de la Cité, a natural stronghold, was the site of a settlement of fishermen and boatmen when the Roman conquerors of Gaul set up a garrison there in the 1st century B.C. They named the place Lutetia Parisiorum, after the Parisii, the Gaulish tribe to which the fishermen and boatmen belonged. The Romans held on to Lutetia and developed it, and by the 4th century A.D. the town had become known as Paris. Much of the early history of Paris is still shrouded in mystery, but the site of Notre-Dame cathedral, the city's most famous religious monument, has always been associated with worship.

The masterpiece of Gothic architecture we can see today was begun in the 12th century by Maurice de Sully, bishop of Paris. Many great moments in French history—royal marriages and baptisms, Te Deums sung to mark great national victories—have been celebrated in this impressive building with its superb rose windows, flying buttresses and slender apse. The poet Charles Péguy once memorably compared it to a great ship anchored in the Seine. Meanwhile, the other end of the Ile de la Cité was becoming established as the seat of the temporal power. It was there that the Romans built a villa for their governor. On the same site the Capetian kings later built a palace which remained a royal residence until the 14th century when it became the headquarters of the *parlement,* the supreme court of law.

The Ile Saint-Louis and the Marais district (literally "the marsh") have had a similar history. Both areas were fertile gardening land which became residential quarters for the aristocracy. The Valois kings began to build on the Marais in the 14th and 15th centuries, and the nobility soon followed suit. At the beginning of the 17th century, Henri IV laid out a spacious square there lined with fine brick and stone houses. In accordance with a custom practised in his native province of the Béarn in southwest France he built shady arcades around the square. Originally called the Place Royale and later renamed **Place des Vosges**, it is one of the most impressive architectural achievements in Paris. Aristocratic town houses were built in the Marais throughout the 17th century. But after this golden age, the nobility began to forsake its narrow bustling streets in favour of the quieter **Ile Saint-Louis** where they settled in magnificent houses such as the Hôtel Lauzun and the Hôtel Lambert on the Quai d'Anjou.

163

semi-fortified royal palace which also housed the king's treasury and a prison. In the early 16th century François I had this fortress razed to the ground and commissioned the architect Pierre Lescot and the sculptor Jean Goujon to build him a magnificent palace on the site with room to house the numerous artists and craftsmen he had engaged to embellish his palaces. Since then the Louvre has had a checkered history. Under Louis XIV it was abandoned and in the 18th century became virtually derelict, finally becoming a museum during the Revolution. Though it contains a fabulous collection of art treasures, it is far from ideal as a museum building, but no major alterations can be made to it since it is a historic monument.

The buildings stretching from the Louvre's inner courtyard, the Cour Carrée, to the Tuileries gardens were only completed during the reign of Napoleon III, the last French ruler to live in the Tuileries Palace, a country house built for Catherine de Medicis in the 16th century. The palace ran at right angles to the Seine and divided the Tuileries gardens from the Place du Carrousel, where Napoleon I erected in 1808 an Arc de Triomphe to commemorate his military successes. Later under Louis-Philippe, the obelisk of Luxor was erected on Place de la Concorde.

In 1871 the Communards burned down the Tuileries Palace and unwittingly opened up the view from one triumphal arch to another. The Tuileries palace was destroyed but **the Tuileries Gardens** remain, with nearby in Place du Carrousel sensuous **bronze statues by Aristide Maillol** put there on the initiative of André Malraux. Paris has other fine perspectives, such as that linking the Champ-de-Mars gardens to the Invalides and **the Montparnasse tower**, as audacious but for the time being more controversial.

The Tuileries Gardens: the Carrousel Arch, the Louvre, and (foreground) a statue by Maillol.

Paris is also a city of spectacular vistas. Some were created by urbanist-kings such as François I, Henri IV and Louis XIII, but the most beautiful of them, like the magnificent view from the Arc de Triomphe to the Louvre, are the result of historical accident rather than deliberate planning. This world-famous prospect, known as the "Voie Triomphale" (triumphal way), stretches from the Arc de Triomphe at the Étoile down the Champs-Élysées, across Place de la Concorde with its obelisk, along the main avenue of the Tuileries gardens to the Arc de Triomphe of the Carrousel and **the Louvre**. Originally a medieval fortress on the banks of the Seine, the Louvre later became a

The Montparnasse Tower.

Montmartre: the Lapin Agile.

Montmartre: the Place du Tertre.

Tower blocks overlooking the Seine.

The obelisk, Place de la Concorde.

The Pont Alexandre III.

Vines once grew on the *Butte,* Montmartre's hillside, and windmill-sails once turned gently in the wind. The millers ran "guinguettes", open-air bars and dance-halls, serving their customers with the bluish, bitter-tasting local wine known as "jinglet". Today **the Place du Tertre**, one of Montmartre's prettiest squares, makes its living from the tourists, but the real "Montmartrois" still live all around in oddly-shaped houses with painted shutters and little gardens which line the steep cobbled streets. From the mid-19th century until well into the 20th, Montmartre was the haunt of all the poets, painters and shady characters in Paris. At the Chat Noir cabaret Aristide Bruant first made his reputation as a writer and singer of vitriolic songs. Renoir set up his easel at the Moulin de la Galette. Toulouse-Lautrec frantically sketched his friends, the dancers of the Moulin-Rouge. Van Gogh painted the Rue Saint-Rustique. And from their home in a wooden building known as the Bateau-Lavoir in the Rue Ravignan a band of wild young men with names like Picasso, Apollinaire, and Max Jacob would emerge to make whoopee with men about **Montmartre** such as Francis Carco and Pierre Mac Orlan at **the Lapin Agile** cabaret (which got its name from an artist named André Gill who painted its sign depicting a rabbit leaping out of a saucepan. It was soon known as Le Lapin à Gill, which was rapidly deformed into *Le Lapin Agile*—the agile rabbit).

While Montmartre was catalyzing Parisian artistic and intellectual life, another, grander Paris was coming into being: the *beaux quartiers,* the residential district on the Right Bank around the Étoile, **the Place de la Concorde** and the Champs-Élysées. **The Pont Alexandre III**, with its splendid wrought-iron lamps and exuberant ornamentation dates from the same period.

It is possible to admire the 56-floor-high Montparnasse Tower as an architectural achievement and still wonder whether it should have been built in the heart of Montparnasse. The Parisians joke about it, but for the moment they do not feel unqualified enthusiasm for it. They are equally unenthusiastic about the new **tower blocks on the bank of the Seine** near the Pont Mirabeau.

Paris has always been made up of a number of villages. You were never simply a Parisian, you were a Parisian from the Gobelins, from Passy, from Auteuil, from Plaisance, from the Bastille, from Belleville, from Bercy, from the Halles or from "La Mouffe" (the Rue Mouffetard). But today the new tower blocks are sounding the death-knell for these unique "village-quarters."

And yet some villages have managed to survive, notably Montmartre, the most famous of them all.

The National Assembly and the fountains
on Place de la Concorde.

The development of the Champs-Élysées and the other elegant residential
and shopping districts on the Right Bank of the Seine largely took place in the
19th century. The Champs-Élysées, originally laid out as formal gardens by Le
Nôtre in the 17th century, only began to take its modern shape with the building of the Arc de Triomphe, which was planned by Napoleon but took 30
years to complete. The pace of development began to quicken in the last quarter of the century. In 1873 the Élysée Palace, an 18th-century mansion standing between the Champs-Élysées and the Faubourg Saint-Honoré, became the
official residence of the French President. Two other landmarks date from the
end of the century: the Petit Palais and its massive glass-domed big brother,
the Grand Palais, which both adjoin the Cours la Reine, a chestnut-covered
riverside promenade laid out by Queen Marie de Médicis in the 17th century.
Meanwhile, other fashionable quarters were coming into being nearby around
the Madeleine, the Opéra, the Rue Royale dominated by the soon-to-be-
famous Maxim's restaurant, Place Vendôme with its great jewellers' shops, the
Faubourg Saint-Honoré with its booksellers, antique dealers, art galleries and
fashion houses. In 1862 work began on the Opéra, symbol of the glittering
world of Second Empire France. Designed by Charles Garnier, the building
was opened in 1875. During the same period another rich residential quarter

The Parc Monceau.

was developing on **the Plaine Monceau**, where luxurious mansions were built around a **pretty park**. The atmosphere in this part of the city has changed little since those days, when Marcel Proust was growing up there. All these fashionable districts, these "beaux quartiers" of Paris which are a little too opulent to be charming, owe their existence directly or indirectly to the work of one man, Baron Haussmann. As Napoleon III's Prefect of the Seine, Haussmann carried out a revolution in city planning in 19th-century Paris, creating the broad avenues known as the Grands Boulevards and making the city a healthier place to live in. Alas, for reasons that often had more to do with politics than urbanism, Haussmann also destroyed some of the city's oldest and most attractive quarters—around Notre-Dame, on the Montagne Sainte-Geneviève, in the Latin Quarter and the Faubourg Saint-Antoine.

It is impossible to do justice to the infinite variety of Paris, with its mosaic of rich quarters and popular quarters, its patchwork of parks and gardens ranging from its two great "lungs", the Bois de Vincennes and the Bois de Boulogne, to the Tuileries gardens, the Champ-de-Mars, the Jardin des Plantes, its "villages" such as Montmartre, Montparnasse, Saint-Germain-des-Prés, its historic monuments, skyscrapers and official buildings like **the National Assembly.** More than anywhere it reflects the diversity of French life.

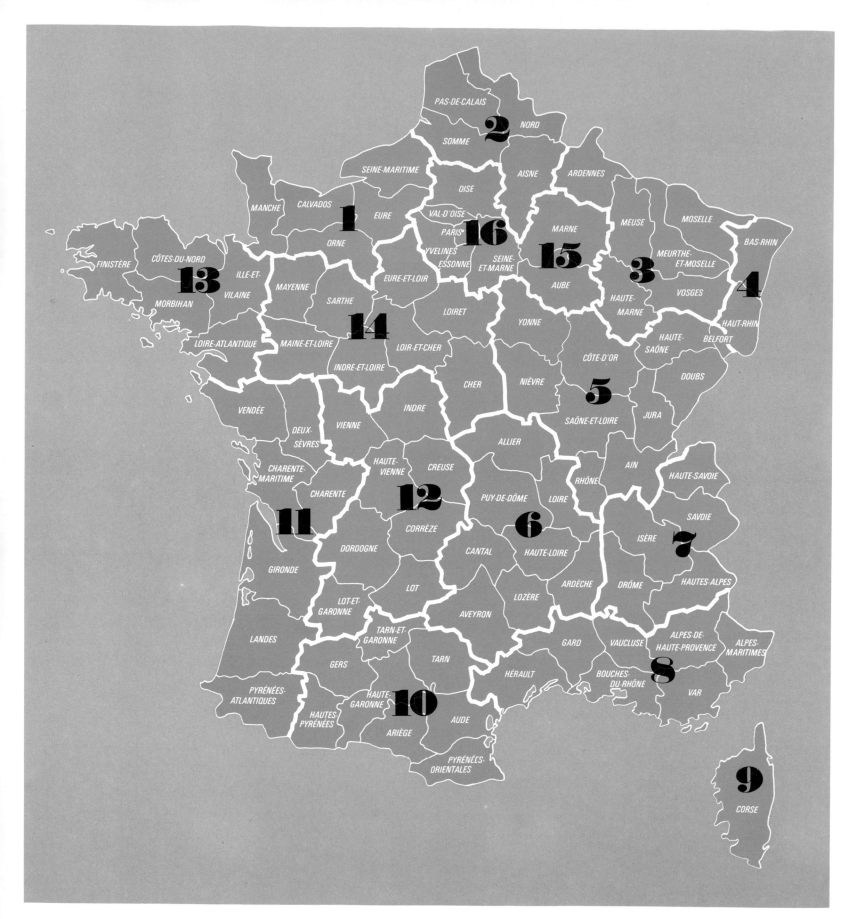

PAS-DE-CALAIS
NORD
SOMME
2
SEINE-MARITIME
AISNE
ARDENNES
OISE
MANCHE
CALVADOS
1
EURE
VAL-D'OISE
MARNE
MEUSE
MOSELLE
ORNE
PARIS*
16
MEURTHE-
ET-MOSELLE
BAS-RHIN
FINISTÈRE
CÔTES-DU-NORD
YVELINES
15
VOSGES
13
ILLE-ET-
MAYENNE
EURE-ET-LOIR
ESSONNE
SEINE-
ET-MARNE
AUBE
3
4
VILAINE
SARTHE
HAUTE-
MARNE
HAUT-RHIN
MORBIHAN
LOIRET
BELFORT
14
HAUTE-
SAÔNE
LOIRE-ATLANTIQUE
MAINE-ET-LOIRE
LOIR-ET-CHER
YONNE
CÔTE-D'OR
DOUBS
INDRE-ET-LOIRE
CHER
NIÈVRE
5
VENDÉE
VIENNE
INDRE
JURA
DEUX-
SÈVRES
SAÔNE-ET-LOIRE
ALLIER
AIN
CHARENTE-
MARITIME
HAUTE-
VIENNE
CREUSE
HAUTE-SAVOIE
RHÔNE
CHARENTE
12
PUY-DE-DÔME
LOIRE
SAVOIE
11
CORRÈZE
6
ISÈRE
7
DORDOGNE
CANTAL
HAUTE-LOIRE
GIRONDE
DRÔME
HAUTES-ALPES
LOT
ARDÈCHE
LOT-ET-
GARONNE
LOZÈRE
AVEYRON
ALPES-DE-
HAUTE-PROVENCE
ALPES-
MARITIMES
LANDES
TARN-ET-
GARONNE
GARD
VAUCLUSE
GERS
TARN
8
HÉRAULT
BOUCHES-
DU-RHÔNE
VAR
PYRÉNÉES-
ATLANTIQUES
HAUTE-
GARONNE
10
AUDE
HAUTES-
PYRÉNÉES
ARIÈGE
9
PYRÉNÉES-
ORIENTALES
CORSE

Appendices

1
NORMANDY

WHERE TO GO

The abbeys of the lower Seine: Between Rouen and the Seine estuary a number of great ruined abbeys are strung along the river valley. The ideal way to see them would be by boat, but failing that we recommend you to take the Route Nationale 182 out of Rouen. First stop is at Saint-Martin-de-Boscherville to see the ruins of the abbey of St. George (founded 1050). Its massive lantern tower is a remarkable example of Norman Romanesque architecture.

Carry on along the N.182 and after passing through Duclair turn left along the D.143 to Jumièges, one of the greatest abbeys in Western Christendom during the Middle Ages. Time and vandals have inflicted harsh treatment on the great Romanesque abbey church; all that remains of it are the façade, flanked by 52-metre-high towers, and most of the nave.

Just before Caudebec (still on the N.182) turn right for Saint-Wandrille. It too is ruined, but majestic columns and arches convey some idea of its former splendour. Since 1931 Benedictine monks have been back at Saint-Wandrille, the new abbey church being housed in a 13th-century barn whose oak woodwork is particularly fine.

At Caudebec take the D.81 for Villequier where Victor Hugo's daughter Léopoldine and her husband Charles Vacquerie were drowned. The home of the Vacquerie family is now a Victor Hugo museum.

From Evreux to Caen: There are several possibilities. One is to take the N.830 out of Evreux and then join the D.140 at Conches. This will take you through the Forest of Conches, through Beaumesnil (magnificent château) to Bernay (basilica of Notre-Dame-de-la-Couture). Then on to Lisieux (D.138 then N.13).

Another possibility is to leave Evreux by the N.13 then take the D.39 for Neubourg (18th-century château of Champ-de-Bataille). Take the D.137 to Brionne then the N.138 and the D.39 to Le Bec-Hellouin (ruins of great medieval abbey). Then on to Lisieux.

After Lisieux you are in Normandy at its most Norman: the Pays d'Auge, with its fruit trees and fat cattle, half-timbered houses and meadows, farms and manors.

To taste the more sophisticated pleasures of Deauville and Trouville, fashionable since the Second Empire, take the N.179 out of Lisieux to Pont-l'Évêque, then the N.834.

The N.813 leads you along the coast westwards to Cabourg, where Proust stayed at the Grand Hôtel and saw the "jeunes filles en fleurs". Then on to Caen, where William the Conqueror and his wife Matilda are buried at the Abbaye aux Hommes and the Abbaye aux Femmes respectively. Visit the castle built by the Conqueror.

Return to the coast from Caen and then make a pilgrimage to the beaches where the allied armies landed in 1944. This will take you through Saint-Lô and Cherbourg to the coast of the Cotentin peninsula, on the border of Brittany. From Avranches the bay of Mont-Saint-Michel can be seen in the distance.

A pleasant trip through eastern Normandy starts at Aumale and follows the valley of the river Bresle to Le Tréport. Then turn west along the coast for a visit to Dieppe, one of France's oldest seaside resorts. Make a small detour to Varengeville, where Monet painted the clifftops in the 1880s and 1890s and where the painter Georges Braque (like Monet a Norman) is buried. Then on to Saint-Valery-en-Caux and the fishing port of Fécamp with its magnificent church of the Trinity.

WHAT TO EAT

Normandy is renowned for its seafood, dairy products, meat and vegetables. It is a region which has everything to satisfy the gourmand as well as the gourmet.

Many Norman towns have a gastronomic speciality. Here are some of them: *Andouille de Vire* (a lightly smoked black-skinned sausage made of pig's innards); *andouillette d'Alençon* (chitterling sausage); *boudin blanc d'Avranches* (white sausage).

Tripe La Ferté-Macé-style is cooked on skewers; *tripes à la mode de Caen* is tripe cooked for hours with ox feet, cider, Calvados, carrots, onions and herbs. Sole cooked *à la Dieppoise* is prepared with cream, white wine, prawns and mussels. Rouen has famous duck dishes made with ducks killed in such a way that they retain their blood, which is squeezed out of the carcase during preparation and used in the sauce. Poulet Vallée d'Auge is chicken cooked in cream. Given the availability of such tempting fare, it is not surprising that meals in old Normandy sometimes lasted a week. (So the story goes.)

Normandy is equally famous for its cheeses: the strong, tangy Livarot and the Pont-l'Évêque with its dark yellow crust fight out an endless and inconclusive battle with Camembert, the aristocrat of Norman cheeses, invented in the early 19th century in the Vallée d'Auge, supposedly by a farmer's wife named Marie Carel.

Delicious cider of varying degrees of sweetness and alcohol content is also produced in Normandy and often drunk with meals instead of wine. If your energy seems to be flagging in the middle of a copious repast, then try the *trou Normand* ("Norman hollow"), a shot of Calvados (Norman apple brandy) which is alleged by many Normans to aid digestion.

FOLK TRADITIONS AND FESTIVALS

When motor vessels replaced sailing boats in the Norman fishing fleets after World War I, the great celebrations which once marked various stages in the fishing season began to die out. The tradition still survives at Fécamp, where the sea and the fishing boats are blessed in mid-January at the "Pardon des Terre-Neuvas".

Whit Sunday is carnival day in Granville, and on Whit Monday the "Charitons", religious brotherhoods which originated as medieval burial societies, make an annual pilgrimage to Notre-Dame-de-la-Couture at Bernay. On the same day there is an open-air Mass in front of the church of Notre-Dame-de-Grâce, which looks out over the Seine estuary and the sea above Honfleur.

The people of Pont-d'Ouilly don traditional costume for the procession of Saint-Rochant, and Lisieux honours its patron saint, St. Theresa, in October. Mortagne-au-Perche holds an annual fair to celebrate its most famous product, *boudin* (black sausage). On the last Sunday in August there is an open-air Mass at the château of Carrouges, when prayers are offered on behalf of hunters to their patron saint, St. Hubert.

2 PICARDY AND ARTOIS

WHERE TO GO

For once don't shun the towns. Interesting ones in the region include Amiens, Cambrai and Soissons, with its ancient abbey of Saint-Jean-des-Vignes. Soissons cathedral, with its remarkable semi-circular transept, deserves a lengthy visit. It was begun in 1177 during the first upsurge of Gothic inspiration.

For centuries this has been one of the most fought-over areas in Europe. Witness the military cemeteries from World War I. At the Caverne du Dragon, on the Chemin des Dames, the hilltop road parallel to the Aisne river east of Soissons that was the scene of General Nivelle's ill-fated offensive in 1917, there is a museum devoted to the fighting.

The ponds and marshes of the Somme valley provide a pleasant, if somewhat melancholy background for an excursion. Visit the *hortillonnages* (see page 17) and the 13th-century château at Péronne. Hangest-sur-Somme commands a magnificent view out over the valley. The bay of the Somme is still magnificently wild and unspoilt.

In the Thiérache region, between the Oise and Sambre rivers, there are a number of interesting fortified churches. Two routes are possible: one from Guise to Hirson, through Beaurin, Marly, Englancourt, Saint-Algis, Autreppes, Vimy and Ohis; the other from Marle to Vernins through Tavaux, Vigneux, Archon, Parfondeval, Dohis, Plomion, Hary, Burelles and Prisces.

Those who like solitude, windswept scenery and a surrealist atmosphere would enjoy a cold, sunny winter weekend walking along the deserted beaches of Picardy's Channel resorts.

WHAT TO EAT

In Picardy, if you ask for a *ficelle* ("a piece of string"), the chef will lovingly prepare a kind of pancake covered with cream, garnished with ham and mushrooms and browned in the oven.

Stop at nothing to get served with a *matelote d'anguilles* (eels stewed in wine) or a succulent eel pâté. Less sophisticated, perhaps, but equally tasty, is the *flamiche* or *flamique,* a cream and leek tart eaten hot from the oven.

Then try one of the local cheeses, the Maroilles (or Marolles) or the Rollot. Marolles is a rich, strong-flavoured cheese, the Rollot a soft cow's-milk cheese with a red rind.

FOLK TRADITIONS AND FESTIVALS

The most picturesque festivals and ceremonies in Picardy take place on the coast and are connected with fishing. In the past the cod fishermen made merry on Shrove Tuesday as part of their preparations for long months of isolation and hard work in the Icelandic fishing grounds. Dunkirk still celebrates this occasion with a carnival known as the *Vischer bende* (literally "band of fishermen") when its streets are thronged with revellers following a brass band led by a drum major wearing the uniform of the Imperial Guard. The same occasion is celebrated at Malo-les-Bains.

May is carnival month at Saint-Quentin, while Saint-Omer holds its "festival of the three hats". Seclin holds a festival in honour of the herring on Trinity Sunday, and in September Cambrai has its annual garlic fair. Each December Maubeuge honours the patron saint of jewellers, St. Éloi.

Giant puppets are paraded through the streets of the towns and cities of the Nord Département at festival time. At Hazebrouck the medieval hero Roland is the central figure, and on the last Sunday in April, John the Woodcutter makes his appearance in the streets of Steenvoorde. On Easter Monday two giant figures known as "Papa Reuze" and "Mama Reuze" are the centrepiece of a parade through the streets of Cassel, and on the Sunday after 5 July giant puppets of the "Gayant" family parade in their 16th-century costumes in Douai.

The *"braderie"* of Lille, an autumn fair held each September, is becoming increasingly famous. The streets are lined with stalls selling everything under the sun.

3
LORRAINE AND CHAMPAGNE

WHERE TO GO

The atmosphere of Lorraine's strife-ridden history can be felt most vividly on a visit to Verdun and the ruined forts outside the town which bore the brunt of the bitter fighting during 1916-1917. The ossuary of Douaumont is a monumental and grisly memorial to the battle.

But Lorraine is a region of contrasts. One side can be seen in industrial towns like Longwy and Thionville, in Lorraine's ironworks and salt-mines, textile mills and hydro-electric power stations; another face of Lorraine is the slopes of the Vosges, an area of rural peace and unspoilt countryside.

Leave Chaumont by the N.65. After Montigny-le-Roi the road crosses the stripling Meuse, just four kms. from its source. Then take the N.417 for Bourbonne-les-Bains to the spa town of Plombières. From Plombières take the N.57 to Remiremont, delightfully situated in the high valley of the Moselle. Cross the Moselle and take the N.417 again. The road then runs alongside the Lakes of Gérardmer and Longemer before climbing to the Col de la Schlucht. Descend the Alsatian slopes of the Vosges, and make a detour to Turckheim before heading for Colmar.

WHAT TO EAT

Lorraine cooking is simple, straightforward and has a long tradition behind it.

There are several specialities. The *potée Lorraine* is a kind of *pot au feu* in which either bacon or salt pork replaces the usual beef. Another Lorraine speciality is a *matelote* (fish stew) of trout or pike. These fish are also prepared in the local *vin gris* or prepared *bleu* (quickly cooked in boiling water or vinegar so that maximum taste and freshness are preserved).

Cheeses: try the Géromé, made on the western slopes of the Vosges. Its flavour is strong, similar to that of Munster.

On a cold day warm yourself up with a tot of plum brandy *(eau-de-vie de Mirabelle)*. The dry wines of Toul and the Moselle should not be ignored on even the shortest gastronomic tour of Lorraine.

FOLK TRADITIONS AND FESTIVALS

Carnival time in Metz and Nancy is halfway through Lent. If you happen to be in the area on Holy Thursday and see a little pine boat bearing a lighted candle float by on a stream then you have witnessed a ceremony of the "Champs-Golots" festival which marks the beginning of Spring. Metz, Lunéville and Nancy hold festivals in honour of the mirabelle plum halfway through August. Joan of Arc is honoured at her birthplace Domrémy and at Nancy on 8 May. Each year on 8 September a procession of pilgrims visits the sanctuary of Notre-Dame-de-Bon-Secours at Sion-Vaudémont, the *Colline inspirée* of Maurice Barrès' book of that title.

4
ALSACE

WHERE TO GO

A leisurely tour of Alsace might include the following itinerary, which will take you from Strasbourg up into the Vosges, along the magnificent Route des Crêtes (a hilltop road built during World War I to ensure communications between the different valleys on the Vosges front) and then back to Strasbourg through the vineyards.

Leave Strasbourg by the autoroute B.35, then take the N.425, with Mount Sainte-Odile in the background. Next take the N.426 to Obernai, a delightful town with typical old Alsatian houses, a corn market and a church with 15th-century stained-glass windows.

As you leave the vineyards, the N.426 starts to rise. You pass through Ottrott, where there is a vineyard producing one of Alsace's few red wines, and two castles, the Lutzelbourg and the Rathsamhausen.

Thirty-six kms. further on is Klingenthal, once famous as the place where French kings had their swords and daggers made. The road now winds through pine trees up to the mountain named after St. Odile, patron saint of Alsace. Born blind, she gained her sight when she was baptised.

Her father, duke of Alsace, gave her the mountain of Hohenbourg where she founded a convent. (It can still be visited.)

Carry on through the woods, vineyards and pretty villages of the Hohwald region, then drive to Sainte-Marie-aux-Mines.

Cross the Col du Bonhomme and continue as far as the calvary of Luschpach, then descend to Colmar via Les Trois Épis and Turckheim.

From Colmar to Cernay, strike back up into the Vosges by the N.417, for Munster, the Route des Crêtes and the highest point in the Vosges, the Grand Ballon de Guebwiller. Then down to Cernay.

The return route to Strasbourg passes through major centres of the Alsatian vineyard: Ammerschwirr, Riquewihr and Ribeauvillé.

Don't miss the castle of Haut-Kœnigsbourg (where Jean Renoir made his famous film *La Grande Illusion*).

WHAT TO EAT

Many people think that Alsatian gastronomy starts and ends with sauerkraut (succulent though it can be) and Munster cheese (with or without caraway seeds). Nothing could be further from the truth. Alsace produces superb *charcuterie—foie gras,* terrines, hams and sausages, as well as tempting desserts.

Alsatian wines are usually named after the grape they are made from rather than the property they are grown on. The Riesling, the Sylvaner, the Traminer, the Gewurztraminer and the Pinot Blanc make an excellent accompaniment to game, which is plentiful in Alsace.

Alsatian cooks are nothing if not imaginative. Try a *Baeckeoffe,* an unlikely mixture of beef, pork and mutton mixed with vegetables and slowly cooked in white wine. Or else order a *Leber Knoedel,* rissoles of pig's and calf's liver seasoned with garlic and onions and simmered in a mixture of flour, eggs and croutons.

Alsace boasts a wide assortment of puddings and cakes including: *Kugelhopf,* a sweet cake containing candied fruit and nuts, baked in a mould; aniseed biscuits; *Eierkuchas,* rich pancakes stuffed with redcurrant jelly. They are all capable of putting the finishing touches to an Alsatian meal, before that last glass of Schnapps or *eau de vie* made from cherries (Kirsch), raspberry, pear, mirabelle plum, quetsche plum, or bilberry...

FOLK TRADITIONS AND FESTIVALS

Mascarades, cavalcades, processions in traditional costume and pilgrimages have always formed part of the Alsatian scene. Sélestat, Mulhouse and Munster make merry on the Sundays before or after Shrove Tuesday. Colmar revives its old traditions at the festival of its old town, Saverne at its rose festival, held every June.

At Thann at the end of June three pine trees are "cremated" in front of the cathedral to commemorate the town's foundation. Most spectacular of all is Ribeauvillé's "Pfifferday", a procession in honour of the Virgin of Dusenbach, patron of the corporation of musicians. The wine harvest is celebrated in wine-growing towns such as Turckheim, Riquewihr, Guebwiller, Barr and Obernai as soon as the grapes are picked.

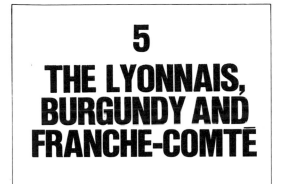

5
THE LYONNAIS, BURGUNDY AND FRANCHE-COMTÉ

WHERE TO GO
See this many-sided region slowly and savour its many attractions.

Firstly architecture: Vézelay, Cluny and Tournus are masterpieces of Romanesque architecture. There are many fine châteaux: Époisses, Saint-Fargeau, Ancy-le-Franc, Tanlay, Bazoches, La Rochepot, Palteau and Le Clos Vougeot are all well worth a visit.

Burgundy is a wonderful part of France, no matter how you choose to get about it, by car or even on horseback, on foot or by boat: try a leisurely tour of the canals. You have a choice between the canals of Burgundy, the Centre, the Nivernais and the Loire.

Particularly beautiful are the Morvan Natural Park, and the lakes: Lac du Crescent, Lac de Saint Agnan, Lac de Pannesières and Lac des Settons. The Jura to the east has many natural attractions: the Forest of the Joux, the source of the Doubs river, the Perte de l'Ain where the Ain river goes underground, the Gorges of Malvaux and La Langouette. Besançon is an ideal base for visiting the valley of the

Doubs around the Lake of Chaillexon and the spectacular waterfalls known as the Saut du Doubs. Further south, Lons-le-Saunier is within easy reach of the Cirque de la Baume and its pretty village of Baume-les-Messieurs, the Cascades du Hérisson and the Col de la Faucille.

At Lyons don't miss the church of St. Martin d'Ainay, the cathedral of Saint-Jean, the palace of Saint-Pierre, the Hôtel de Ville and the Hôtel-Dieu.

WHAT TO EAT
Burgundy, Franche-Comté and the Lyonnais are famed for the quality of their cooking and the wide variety of dishes. The charcuterie in particular has a high reputation. The *judru* sausage from Chagny in the Côte d'Or, the rosette from Chalon, the *jésus* from Morteau and the Lyonnais truffled *cervelas en brioche*.

There is plenty of freshwater fish: Loire trout, pike from the Saône, the delicious *pôchouse* or freshwater fish stew from Verdun-sur-le-Doubs and Lyonnais carp with cream.

It would be a pity to visit Burgundy without tasting the snails, or Bresse without tasting the famous frogs. Bresse also produces fine chicken: at Brou market you can see them being sold every week. A few more dishes not to be missed are the Burgundy-style fricassée of chicken, cockerel cooked in Chambertin, hare stew in Pommard and woodcock salmis garnished with mushrooms.

In Lyons try pike quenelles with crayfish butter and the gratin of crayfish tails. These dishes never taste the same elsewhere.

There is a wide variety of cheese: in Burgundy the Époisses (prepared with cloves and fennel) and the Cîteaux; in the high Jura the Comté and blue cheese; blue cheese from Bresse; Cancoillotte (soft, strong cheese) from Franche-Comté; from the Lyons area the Saint-Marcellin, the Fourme de Montbrison and the Rigotte de Condrieu. In days gone by the people of Lyons were particularly fond of "fromage fort", a strongly seasoned mixture of the remains of goat's milk cheeses softened in white wine. The *Vacherin du Mont d'Or* is a delicious soft cheese eaten in the Jura.

Many of the greatest wines of France come from this area, from Burgundy, the Jura and the Loire. To name but a few: Chablis, Beaune, Gevrey-Chambertin, Chambolle-Musigny, Pommard, Mercurey, Givry, Rully, Pouilly-Fuissé, Arbois, Château-Chalon.

FOLK TRADITIONS AND FESTIVALS
On the last Sunday in January, all the wine-growing communes hold ceremonies in honour of the patron saint of wine-growers, Saint Vincent. On May 31 at Semur-en-Auxois takes place the oldest organized horse race in France, called the Course de la Bague, which was first run in 1339. On the third Saturday, Sunday and Monday in November are celebrated the Trois Glorieuses de Bourgogne at Clos-Vougeot, Beaune and Meursault.

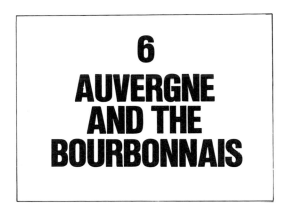

6
AUVERGNE AND THE BOURBONNAIS

WHERE TO GO
Leave Le Puy by the N.88 for a trip across the Cévennes of the Vivarais. At Le Pont de Peyrard, the D.36 starts to rise towards the Mézenc, a grassy plateau of volcanic origin. Drive as far as Les Estables, one of the highest villages in the centre of France. Leave your car there and then take the hour and a half's walk to the summit of the Mézenc, the highest point of the Vivarais Cévennes.

Back in Les Estables, get your breath back at the châlet-hôtel of Le Gerbier-de-Jonc, near the source of the Loire. A few hundred metres away the D.116 rejoins the N.535. A slight detour on the D.16 will take you to Lake d'Issarles. Then visit the lovely Renaissance chapel at Le Monastier-sur-Gazeille before returning to Le Puy by the N.535.

WHAT TO EAT
The Auvergnats have to put up a tough fight against hard winters, and food is one of their major weapons.

Culinary delights are prepared in summer to bring pleasure to the dark winter months. The Massif Central, the high plateaux of the Ardèche, the Cantal and the Rouergue have a name for *charcuterie*. Aurillac is noted for its *tripoux*, mutton or veal tripe simmered in seasoned stock and wine sauce. The Rouergue makes a kind of fondue known as *aligot,* a mixture of mashed potatoes, melted cheese, garlic, butter, pork fat and milk.

Auvergne cheeses include Cantal, the spicy, blue-veined Fourme d'Ambert, and the *bleu d'Auvergne.*

There are few vineyards in Auvergne, but enough to produce two delicious wines, the Châteaugay and the Saint-Pourçain.

FOLK TRADITIONS AND FESTIVALS
They are mainly religious in inspiration and show a marked taste for the grandiose and the theatrical.

Each Good Friday, Burzet in the Ardèche reconstitutes the Passion of Christ. In a ceremony whose origins go back to the 13th century, there is a procession up to the church of the Calvary by a path marked by 32 stations of the Cross decorated with primitive paintings.

A celebrated statue of a Black Virgin, the object of many pilgrimages, is kept during the winter at Besse-en-Chandesse. In accordance with a tradition that goes back to the 17th century, on 2 July it is carried in procession to the church of Notre-Dame-de-Vassivière in the little village of Vassivière. It is returned to Besse on the evening of the Sunday following 21 September.

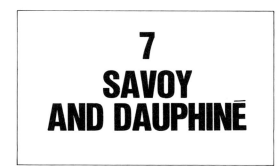

7
SAVOY
AND DAUPHINÉ

WHERE TO GO
There is plenty to see around the historic town of Chambéry. At nearby Les Charmettes you can still see an old house with white walls and green shutters where Jean-Jacques Rousseau stayed. On the banks of the Lac du Bourget is the 12th-century Abbaye de Hautecombe which inspired the 19th-century French Romantic poet Lamartine to write one of his most famous poems, *Le Lac.*

The road through the high Alps is a source of constant fascination for the tourist with fine views as it twists and turns through the high peaks in a landscape of sparkling snow and ice. Cross over into

Italy by way of Chamonix and the Mont Blanc tunnel, which will take you to Courmayeur. Return over the Col du Petit Saint Bernard, the Iseran and the Galibier. Or remain in France and enjoy similar breathtaking Alpine scenery in the Tarentaise. From Grenoble take the interesting but sometimes tricky Route des Grands Cols. It climbs up through the Gorges de la Romanche, the Maupas pass and the Col de la Croix de Fer, passing through the Galibier, the Lautaret, the upper gorges of the Romanche and Bourg d'Oisans.

On the Vercors plateau—a refuge for the French Resistance during the Second World War—there are some fine sites, for example la Combe-Laval between Saint-Jean en Royans and Pont en Royans.

The Massif de la Chartreuse is used as a retreat by the Grande Chartreuse monks, so visitors are not allowed to enter, but you might be interested to know that the nearby distillery where the monks make Chartreuse liqueur from a secret recipe is open to visitors.

WHAT TO EAT
The cooking in the Alps is simple and healthy. The local smoked, dried ham, trout and crayfish from the mountain streams and a bewildering variety of mushrooms are welcome in the chilly mountain evenings. Follow them with local cheeses: Tomme (the Combe de Savoie version is coated with brandy), Reblochon, Vacherin (which in the Drôme and the Isère is laden with parsley), Saint Marcellin (with its distinctive blue-mould crust), Chevrotin (goat's milk cheese) and Sassenage blue cheese. In fact there is a huge selection of excellent cheeses as one might expect in a pastureland area.

There are many local wines, despite the altitude: Roussette from Frangy and Seyssel, Crépy (white wine), Marin, Ripaille, Chignin, Abymes (red and white wines), Montmélian (all from Savoy). From the area where the mountains slope down to the plain comes the Clairette de Die, a sparkling white wine which should be eaten with a special local brioche: the *pogne* from the nearby town of Romans.

FOLK TRADITIONS AND FESTIVALS
There is a lot going on in the Alps throughout the year. In June there is a vintage car rally at Annecy followed by a costume competition. At the end of June, also in Annecy, there is an international festival of cartoon films. At the beginning of July the old part of Aix-les-Bains holds its festival. In mid-July, an international Al-

pine folklore festival at Chambéry. Also in mid-July, a festival in the old quarter of Faverges near Annecy. Slightly later at Clusaz, also near Annecy, a festival of gastronomy, particularly celebrating the Reblochon cheese.

At the beginning of August Flumet holds its traditional mule and foal market.

And at Christmas and the New Year, there are torchlight descents by ski instructors in the winter sports resorts.

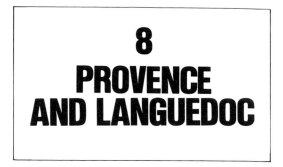

8
PROVENCE
AND LANGUEDOC

WHERE TO GO
A good way to see Provence is to follow in Napoleon's footsteps. In other words take the "Route Napoléon", the road he took when he marched from the Mediterranean to Paris on his return from Elba. The road leads from Cannes to Grasse, Castellane, Digne and Sisteron. Napoleon went mostly on foot, using a walking stick. From Sisteron the road takes you to Gap and Grenoble, through some of the finest scenery of the mountainous *arrière-pays* of Provence. Whether you set off from Cannes, Nice or Draguignan, don't miss a visit to the spectacular gorges of the Verdon, a Grand Canyon in miniature.

Avignon makes an ideal base for a tour of inland Provence. It is a beautiful old walled city dominating the Rhône. A celebrated festival of theatre and dance is held each summer in the 14th-century Palais des Papes and elsewhere. Make a tour of the Luberon mountains and their peaceful villages.

From Avignon you can head south towards the Rhône delta, stopping off at Arles and Saint-Rémy-de-Provence (remains of the Gallo-Roman town of Glanum 2 km from Saint-Rémy). From Arles make a tour of the wild Camargue plain, ending up at the gypsies' town of Saintes-Marie-de-la-Mer.

Northwest of Arles are Nîmes and the famous Roman aqueduct known as the Pont du Gard, set in a landscape of parched limestone hills which are known locally as *garrigues.*

WHAT TO EAT

Provençal cooking is nothing if not colourful. It is also tasty through copious use of spices, herbs and olive oil.

Marseilles is synonymous with *bouillabaisse.* Every native of coastal Provence has his own authentic recipe for this superb fish stew, each one different from the rest. A true *bouillabaisse* in fact contains a variety of Mediterranean fish such as the *rascasse,* red mullet and sometimes lobster, crabs and other shellfish. Olive oil and saffron are also essential ingredients. Another traditional Provençal dish is pistou soup, made with tomatoes, green beans, stock, herbs and pasta. There are several versions of *salade Niçoise,* depending on the season, but hard-boiled eggs, anchovies, black olives and tomatoes are constant ingredients.

Try the onion and anchovy tart called the *pissaladière,* and a *panbagna,* a piece of bread soaked in olive oil and garnished with tomatoes, anchovies and olives. Another delicious vegetable dish is *ratatouille,* a stew of aubergines, peppers and courgettes.

You might also sample fried suppions (small squid) and octopus *à la Niçoise,* served with a peppery tomato sauce. *Pieds et paquets,* calf's feet wrapped in tripe and cooked in a spicy white wine and tomato sauce, is a Marseilles speciality. Quintessentially Provençal is *aioli,* garlic-flavoured mayonnaise often served with fish, seafood or vegetables. Accompany your Provençal meals with Provençal wines: cool Côtes de Provence rosé or the wine of Bandol.

FOLK TRADITIONS AND FESTIVALS

Carnivals in Provence seem to take place at the drop of a hat, thanks to the sunshine, the ebullient Mediterranean temperament and the presence of a strong folk tradition. Nice has its celebrated flower carnival in February, the same month that Menton holds its lemon festival, when floats laden with oranges and lemons are driven through the streets. In June Tarascon, between Arles and Avignon, celebrates its legendary monster Tarasque. Half man, half fish, it devoured the people of Tarascon until tamed by St. Martha.

In October the gypsies congregate at Saintes-Maries-de-la-Mer on a pilgrimage in honour of their patron saint, St. Sarah. Marseilles and Arles exhibit traditional carved figures called *santons* in December. The Christmas midnight Mass at Les Baux-de-Provence is simple and moving.

All through the summer many villages in the Bouches-du-Rhône and Gard Départements hold fêtes with bullfights and competitions whose aim is to snatch a rosette from between a bull's horns. There are bullfights at Arles every Easter; at Nîmes at Whitsun. Special bullfights in both towns are held on the last Sunday in September to celebrate the wine-harvest. Arles' July festival is now accompanied with a music and theatre festival. Other festivals in Provence: at Avignon, Orange and Aix in July; the Cannes film festival in May.

9
CORSICA

WHERE TO GO

If your starting point is Ajaccio, Napoleon's birthplace, there are several possible routes you might choose to tour the island: Leave the coast behind and take the road inland towards Corsica's ancient capital, Corte. The N.193 climbs steeply among the chestnut forests of Bocognano up to the Col de Vizzavona, a health resort on the edge of the mountains.

If you prefer to keep to the coast, follow the N.199 with views over the gulfs of Sagone, Porto and Girolata along to Calvi and Cap Corse, the northernmost point of the island.

Continue your trip along the eastern coast of the island, through the former capital of Bastia, the wine-growing centre of Aleria and Porto Vecchio until you reach Bonifacio, the southernmost point of the island.

If you then wish to return to Ajaccio, take the road to Sartène (N.196). If you change your mind en route, turn off for Aullène, Zicavo and Ghisoni, and spend some time in Corte.

WHAT TO EAT

Traditional Corsican cooking is determined by the island's geography. Along the coast, there is abundant seafood: sea urchins and crayfish, red mullet and mostelles, which are used to make fine bouillabaisse. In the mountains and maquis, game is plentiful: partridges, woodcock, blackbird pâté and wild boar cooked in Corsican wine with a chestnut sauce.

From the domestic pig comes smoked shoulder, smoked fillet *(lonzo)* and liver sausages *(figatelli).*

There is a variety of Corsican cheeses, the best known being the Broccio, which is often eaten with chestnut fritters, figs and mint-flavoured omelette. With it drink white or rosé wine from Patrimonio or the Ajaccio hills.

FOLK TRADITIONS AND FESTIVALS

Of the traditional ceremonies which are still practised in Corsica today, many are religious in origin.

On Good Friday processions take place in almost every Corsican town, perhaps the most remarkable being that of the Sartène, the *Catenacciu:* each year a penitent is chosen from a secret list of people wanting to play the role of Christ in the procession. Once chosen he is dressed in a red robe with a hood over his face to conceal his identity. He carries a heavy wooden cross through the streets of the town. Behind him four penitents dressed in black bear the dead body of Christ. The bright colours, the impressive solemnity of the participants and the beautiful singing make this a uniquely poignant ceremony.

Also on Good Friday, there are other pilgrimages to be seen at Erbalunga near to Bastia, at Bonifacio, Calvi and Cargèse.

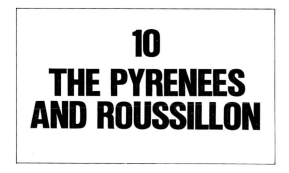

10
THE PYRENEES AND ROUSSILLON

WHERE TO GO

To see some fine examples of the southern French version of Romanesque architecture, take the road out of Perpignan which goes through Villefranche, Bourg-Madame, Corneilla-de-Conflent, Saint-Martin-du-Canigou, Saint-Michel-de-Cuxa and Serrabone. Further along the road are more masterpieces at Elne, Le Boulou, Saint-Martin-de-Fenouillet, Arles-sur-Tech and Coustouges.

Starting out from Toulouse, there are two possibilities. Firstly, a visit to the Albigensian country, starting with the château at Rabastens-sur-Tarn then going on towards Albi and the quadruple ramparts of Cordes. Next go through the Aveyron gorges to Montauban. After Montauban you come to the Montagne Noire and Castres, the Sidobre area where the earth has been eroded to leave huge chaotic heaps of stones, Mazamet and—well protected by its forty-eight towers—the town of Carcassonne.

Within the Ariège area, an unusual experience is a trip underground following the course of the longest subterranean river in the world, at Labouiche. Emerge into the sunshine at Foix and then set off up to Montségur where the Cathar heretics made a desperate last resistance to the crusaders in 1244. Don't leave the region without visiting the Carolingian cave church at Vals.

WHAT TO EAT
The cooking in south-western France is as original and attractive as the ancient monuments. Try the *pot-au-feu* with stuffed fowl; the *ouillade,* garlic soup with eggs; and the *bajanat,* a soup made from dried chestnuts. More traditional is the *charcuterie* with pork-liver sausages, Pézenas *pâtés,* and preserved goose and duck. Sample the seafood: Banyuls *civet de langouste* (lobster and tomato stew), the *sardinade,* the *moulade* and the *bouillinade.*

But don't neglect the local meat dishes, particularly the *cassoulet* or bean stew in its Toulouse, Carcassonne or Castelnaudary versions, and the Cerdagne partridges served with morels. Among the wines of south-west France are Minervois, the Coteaux de Languedoc, Banyuls, Rivesaltes, and the Blanquette de Limoux, a light, sparkling white wine.

FOLK TRADITIONS AND FESTIVALS
The sun-soaked south-west of France is particularly rich in local traditions. On Good Friday in Perpignan, for example, the pilgrims dress the church statues up in theatrical costumes.

Some fascinating and unusual summer events. At Carcassonne there is the "Danse des Mariés" and the "Promenade de l'Ane" and in August the "Promenade du Poulain" through the streets of Pézenas.

Bullfighting is a local passion which has crossed the mountains from Spain with corridas throughout the year, particularly at Collioure and Céret.

11
THE ATLANTIC COAST

WHERE TO GO
A spectacular Pyrenean circuit running through the Aspe and Ossau valleys will take you through Oloron-Sainte-Marie, Sarrance and the Pyrenees National Park. Cross the Col du Somport for a lightning visit to Jaca in Spain then return to France via the Col du Pourtalet, Les Eaux-Chaudes and Laruns.

Then make for the Atlantic and starting from the Basque country follow the Côte d'Argent ("Silver Coast"). Visit Biarritz, Bayonne and Saint-Jean-de-Luz.

Follow the Garonne to Bordeaux, visiting on the way the château de Labrède, birthplace of the 18th-century philosopher Montesquieu, and Langon, the setting of François Mauriac's novel *Genitrix.*

The triangle of land between the Loire, the Gironde and the Atlantic is rich in tourist attractions such as the romantic marshes of Poitou, the historic seaport of La Rochelle, and the offshore islands of Yeu, Noirmoutier, Ré and Oléron.

At Pouzauges, Bressuire, Parthenay, Vouvant, Fontenay-le-Comte, Luçon and Talmont in the *bocage* of the Vendée you will be following the traces of the 18th-century royalist rebels known as the *Chouans.* Before visiting Cognac, make a detour to the north-east and see the Renaissance château of La Rochefoucauld.

Along the northern side of the Gironde estuary, stretching virtually to the ocean, are soft, pleasant, grape-covered hills producing red and white wines. They have been cultivated since the days of the Romans. Pleasant holiday resorts on the Gironde estuary include Saint-Palais-sur-Mer, Pontaillac and Royan.

WHAT TO EAT
The Atlantic coast offers many mouth-watering gastronomic specialities. Here are some of them.

In the Bordeaux region: *tourin,* a rich onion soup thickened with egg yolks; in the Gironde: sautéed eels; in the Landes: preserved goose, duck and pork, *pré-sales* (young sheep pastured on salt marshes), salmis of doves and buntings (the birds are part-roasted then cooked with truffles, mushrooms and white wine and served on sautéed bread with pâté); oysters from the bay of Arcachon.

Basque specialities include *tourri* (onion and tomato soup), *pipérade,* and chicken *à la Basquaise,* served with casseroled potatoes, boletus and chopped Bayonne ham.

The oysters of Marennes in the Charentes are renowned; *chaudrée* is the La Rochelle variant of *bouillabaisse.* In the Poitou marshes try a *matelote* of eels known as a *bouilliture.*

The Bordeaux region is one of the most famous wine-producing areas in the world. There are five principal districts: Graves, Médoc and Sauternes (on the southern bank of the Gironde) and Pomerol and St. Emilion on the northern bank. Among the great red wines: Château Margaux, Château Haut-Brion, Château Latour; the great sweet white wine of the region is Château d'Yquem.

Not to be ignored is Irouléguy, grown close to the Spanish frontier behind Bayonne at the foot of the Pyrenees, the wine of Jurançon in the Béarn, and the red wines of Madiran. The Gironde, the Aunis, the Saintonge and the Angoumois also produce good local wines. The Pineau des Charentes, the wines of the Deux-Sèvres and the *blancs de blanc* of the Vendée have many admirers.

Finally, this is the region where the great French brandies are produced: Cognac and Armagnac.

FOLK TRADITIONS AND FESTIVALS
Blessing of the boats at Arcachon in the second half of March. On 3 June Saint-Emilion celebrates its picturesque "Fête de la Jurade" and on 23 September proclaims the opening of the wine-harvest.

Among the cultural events in the region: La Rochelle's festival of contemporary art and music in May; a festival of ancient music at Saintes in July; and Bordeaux's contemporary art festival (Sigma) in October.

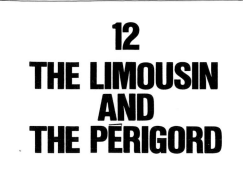

12
THE LIMOUSIN AND THE PÉRIGORD

WHERE TO GO

Périgueux is a good base for several possible trips, providing an impression of the Périgord's wealth of natural and architectural beauty.

The first route is to follow the valley of the Dronne. Take the N.139 out of Périgueux as far as Brantôme, then take the D.78 which follows the Dronne, occasionally cutting across its meanders. At Bourdeilles follow the valley down as far as the crossroads with the D.2; then turn left along the D.2. From Chancelade you are back on the road to Périgueux.

For the second trip, perhaps richer in tourist attractions, take the N.89 then the N.710 to Bugue, where you get onto the N.703 which winds along the Vézère towards the Dordogne. At the top of the Petit-Bout hill, having crossed the Vézère, drive along the Dordogne valley on the D.49 rather than take the direct route for Sarlat. At Saint-Cyprien take the N.703 again, heading for Sarlat via Beynac, La Roque-Gageac and Domme. Take the N.704 from Sarlat to Les Eyzies (near an important prehistoric site), crossing the Enéa valley near Montignac. At Chambon the D.67 winds through the valley of the Nauze and crosses Auriac-du-Périgord. From Thenon return to Périgueux by the N.89.

WHAT TO EAT

Limousin goes in for sober, serious cooking with the *potée* a favourite dish. This excellent peasant meal is just the thing after a day in the open air.

Quercy and the Périgord boast some of the most delicious cooking in France. The region is famed for its truffles and the quality of its duck and pork. Among fish dishes try carp stuffed with *foie gras,* mullet cooked in red wine, crayfish stew, *ballotines* (game and meat boned, stuffed and roast), galantines, chicken *en croûte* served with salsifies. Truffles, along with

foie gras, are the Perigourdine speciality *par excellence*, but other mushrooms hold an honoured place in Périgord cooking: morels, oronges, and flap mushrooms *(cèpes)* stuffed or flavoured with garlic, parsley or grape juice.

The local wines match the quality of the food. Try the light red wines of the Limousin and the wine of Cahors, velvety, full-blooded and dry. Talleyrand claimed that Monbazillac wine was the best to drink with *foie gras*.

FOLK TRADITIONS AND FESTIVALS

Many of the ceremonies and festivals which survive in the Limousin date back almost to the beginning of the Christian era. Every seven years, on the Thursday halfway through Lent, relics of St. Martial are carried in procession. This tradition goes back to the year 1000 when its aim was to exorcise the plague then raging in the Limousin.

Several villages in the Haute-Vienne Département, such as Saint-Léonard-de-Noblat, hold religious festivals whose origins are as ancient.

13
BRITTANY

WHERE TO GO

Don't attempt too much at a time if you want to appreciate this unique part of France properly. One possibility is to set off from Mont-Saint-Michel towards Saint-Brieuc. Stop and visit the magnificent cathedral of Dol-de-Bretagne close by the marshland of Dol. If you want to follow the coast, go shrimp-collecting at Cancale and then sunbathe on the beach at Paramé-Rothéneuf. Visit Saint-Malo and then follow the Rance along to Combourg, where Chateaubriand spent his youth.

On the coast, is Saint-Jacut-de-la-Mer, a charming little fishing village. The D.16 will take you to Fort-de-la-Latte and Cap Fréhel, whose austere beauty contrasts strongly with the soft beaches of Sables d'Or-les-Pins and Val-André. From Perros-Guirec, spend a day visiting Kermaria where there is a sculpted fresco showing a *danse macabre* which reputedly served as inspiration for Saint-Saens. Then go on

to Paimpol and take the boat across to the Ile de Bréhat.

Go and see the pink rocks of Ploumanac'h to the west of Perros Guirec or strike inland and visit the grey cathedral of Tréguier, or the Sept-Saints chapel close to Lannion. If you are beginning your tour of Brittany from Brest, there are other possibilities. You should first of all see the roadsteads of Brest, the Pointe-Saint Mathieu and the Ile d'Ouessant. A little further on are the *abers*, the French version of the Norwegian fjords, where there are beautiful little fishing villages.

At Carnac, a "must" are the lines of menhirs, a relic of Brittany's mysterious Celtic past. See the Gulf of Morbihan, leaving from Vannes, and if possible visit the Ile aux Moines and the Ile de Gavrinis with its huge tumulus containing engraved tablets.

After appreciating the beauties of the coast strike inland to the Argoat, the country of the interior, a fine landscape of moorlands and forests. West of Rennes, for example, is the huge forest of Paimpont which has been identified as the forest of Brocéliande which figures in the ancient stories of the Round Table.

WHAT TO EAT

You should, of course, sample the fine seafood. You will find every imaginable variety from the everyday to the rare and expensive. Grey shrimps, *tourteaux* (crabs), spider crabs *(araignées)*, and also crayfish and lobsters.

Brittany boasts twenty-two growths of Muscadet, so there is a good choice of local wines to accompany meals. If you prefer cider, you again have a wide choice: cider from Loudéac, Dinan, Ploërmel, Fouesnant, etc.

FOLK TRADITIONS AND FESTIVALS

The past is intensely alive in Brittany, as is the old Breton language.

First of all the *pardons*, the religious services for fishermen: the Saint Yves service at Tréguier (May 19), the Notre-Dame-de-tout-Remède service at Rumengol on Trinity Sunday and the Notre-Dame-d'Espérance service at Saint-Brieuc on May 31. Notre-Dame des Naufragés is invoked at the Pointe de Raz on the third Sunday in July, and Sainte-Anne at Sainte-Anne-la-Palud on the last Sunday in August.

As for non-religious events, there is the strawberry festival at Plougastel-Daoulas (3rd Sunday in June) and the apple-tree festival at Fouesnant (3rd Sunday in July).

14
THE LOIRE VALLEY

WHERE TO GO

Don't miss the experience of seeing at least one of the Loire châteaux by night, floodlit for a Son et Lumière show. Châteaux offering Son et Lumière include Loches, Chambord, Amboise, Azay-le-Rideau, Chenonceaux and Angers.

On the boundaries of the Loire valley, Normandy and Brittany is Maine, a forested upland area culminating in the 417-metre-high Mont des Avaloirs, the highest point in Western France. The river valleys, in particularly that of the Mayenne, are spectacularly deep, edged with high cliffs.

On the way to Laval, stop over at Sainte-Suzanne with its imposing ramparts and 11th-century keep. Lassay has a fine fortress built in the mid 15th century. Mézangers boasts the finest building in the whole region: the château du Rocher, a jewel in pure Renaissance style. Laval has a keep and a 12th-century chapel.

Rising out of the Beauce plain is the town of Chartres, whose cathedral has few rivals in France for elegant architecture, stained-glass windows and statues. Wander along the streets of the old town and see the wash-houses on the banks of the Eure, the tanneries and the fortifications, which today stand guard over nothing more dangerous than the town market gardens. From the town gates the Beauce stretches out. It is not simply a flat plain, but a rolling landscape of forests with here and there charming little market towns like Brou and Illiers, where Proust spent much of his childhood.

The Loiret provides a first taste of the Loire landscape. Briare, Gien and Sully-sur-Loire prefigure the luminous skies of Anjou. At Saint-Benoît-sur-Loire the ancient druids used to hold their assemblies. At Germigny-les-Prés stop and admire the Carolingian church and the 9th-century Byzantine-style mosaic consisting of 130,000 different pieces.

Orleans, rebuilt after the war, still remembers its delivery from the English by Joan of Arc in 1429: a museum has been erected in her honour. Visit the source of the Loiret, a resurgence of the Loire which reappears at Olivet and flows alongside the Loire for 12 km before rejoining it.

Afterwards go on to the Sologne forests, a paradise for huntsmen.

WHAT TO EAT

Many fine dishes in the Touraine, Anjou and Orleanais are based on freshwater fish from the Loire: pike, shad and eels are served with succulent sauces. Particularly delicious is the *beurre blanc* sauce, a Loire speciality prepared from a reduction of shallots, white wine vinegar and fresh butter.

The nineteenth-century French novelist, Honoré de Balzac—who particularly loved it—has given us this definition of *rillons*: "Residue of pork sautéed in fat, which look like cooked truffles." You can still enjoy it in the Loire today.

Another delicacy is fricassée of chicken (chicken cooked in stock) served with mushrooms. Follow this with a selection from the local cheeses: Chavignol, Loches, Sainte-Maure and the pyramid-shaped Valençay, whose distinctive flavour comes from being matured in ashes.

The Loire valley produces some fine wines, particularly rosé and white: Vouvray, Savennières, Coulée de Serrant and Jasnière. If you particularly like red wine try Chinon, Bourgueil or Saint-Nicolas-de-Bourgueil.

FOLK TRADITIONS AND FESTIVALS

Each year on May 8 Orleans remembers Joan of Arc who delivered the town from the English in 1429 with a procession to the cross erected in her honour. Two centuries later Louis XIII put France under the protection of the Virgin Mary. This ceremony is still re-enacted each year in Orleans on May 28.

A thoroughly modern French tradition is the 24-hour car race at Le Mans which takes place every year.

Saumur is the home of a famous military riding school, founded in 1764. The officers who are riding instructors in the school constitute the Cadre Noir, whose displays of elegant riding are famous throughout France.

15
THE ILE-DE-FRANCE

WHERE TO GO

Africa awaits you just a few kilometres outside Paris in the form of the nature reserve at the château of Thoiry where lions, monkeys, antelopes and other wild animals roam at liberty in a park and gaze curiously at the visitors driving through. Don't get out of the car whatever you do. The animals are well-fed but they have unpredictable and eclectic appetites.

Forty-seven km north-east of Paris to Ermenonville and you're in the Arizona desert. It's a sandy part of the park of Ermenonville with, nearby... another zoo.

It's possible to take cruises not only on the Seine but on other rivers in the Ile-de-France, the Oise and the Marne. The Sentier de Grande Randonnée is a well-marked walkers' trail that runs 600 km through the countryside in a great circle around Paris. (The trail is indicated by trees marked with red and white paint.) One can join the trail at various points, such as Saint-Germain-en-Laye, accessible by express Metro.

WHAT TO EAT

Ile-de-France cooking is traditional; there are no particular specialities but that doesn't mean the food isn't good. It is. The region abounds in market gardens and orchards, there is plenty of freshwater fish, game and butcher's meat.

FOLK TRADITIONS AND FESTIVALS

The proximity of a great city has not sapped the life out of the folk traditions of the Ile-de-France. St. Sebastian, patron saint of archers, is honoured in many parts of the area during January. In May Conflans-Sainte-Honorine, the great barge centre of the Ile-de-France, holds a Breton-style *pardon*. (See "Folk traditions and festivals" for Brittany.)

Finally, all through the summer, there are Son et Lumière shows at the great châteaux of the Ile-de-France such as Senlis, Chantilly, Grosbois, Moret-sur-Loing, Houdon and above all Versailles (from May to September).

16
PARIS

WHAT TO SEE

Start with a river promenade, either on foot or on one of the pleasure boats known as ''bateaux-mouches''. As you proceed downstream from the tip of the Ile Saint-Louis, you will see some of these bridges and monuments unfold before you:

Left Bank	Islands and bridges	Right Bank
The Jardin des Plantes (zoo and gardens)		Quai Henri-IV
	The Ile Saint-Louis	
	The Ile de la Cité	The Hôtel de Ville
	Notre-Dame cathedral	
	The Hôtel-Dieu	
	The Conciergerie	
	The Sainte-Chapelle	
The Hôtel de la Monnaie (the mint)	The Pont Neuf	
	Statue of King Henri IV	The church of St. Germain-l'Auxerrois
The Institut		The Louvre
		The Tuileries gardens
The National Assembly	The Pont de la Concorde	Place de la Concorde
The Invalides	The Pont Alexandre-III	The Grand and the Petit Palais
	The Pont de l'Alma	Museum of Modern Art
The Eiffel Tower	The Pont d'Iéna	The Palais de Chaillot
The Champ-de-Mars		
The École Militaire		
Seine-side tower blocks	The Ile aux Cygnes	French radio building

Take the Place des Vosges as the starting point for a walk round the narrow, labyrinthine streets of the Marais quarter, with its noble 17th-century mansions and colourful artisans' workshops.

Then wander round the Latin Quarter, on the Left Bank, a little further downstream. Take a steep uphill walk along the Rue Saint-Jacques to the Panthéon, where France's great figures are buried. Then saunter down from Montagne Sainte-Geneviève through the colourful market stalls of the Rue Mouffetard.

PHOTOGRAPHERS

J.-P. Augerot: 79
B. Barbey (Magnum): 147 below
B. Beaujard: 117 below, 147 above, 157
B. Beaujard (Rapho): 57
P. Bérenger: 42 below left, 43 below, 119 left
E. Berne (Fotogram): 50 above, 107, 124 below, 153 above right, 162 above and below
B. Biraben (Rapho): 116
J.-L. Blanchet (Pitch): 111 above
R. Bonnefoy (Top): 142
E. Boubat (Top): 84 below left, 169
J. Boulas: 17, 125, 139, 149, 168
M. Brelet (Top): 121
M. Breton: 88
R. Burri (Magnum): 55 above and below
Carmagnol: 83
H. Cartier-Bresson (Magnum): 132 below
H. Chapman (Fotogram): 90 left
J.-Ph. Charbonnier (Top): 90 right
S. Chirol: 30, 31, 46, 73 below, 94 below, 97, 99 below right, 103
A. Dagbert (Viva): 19, 22 above, 117 above right
R. Delvert: 143
M. Desjardins (Top): 102, 129, 154 above
R. Doisneau (Rapho): 150 left
J. Dubois: 134, 155 left
G. Ehrmann (Top): 65
J. Feuillie: 48, 130
C. Février (Top): 11
G. Fleury (Fotogram): 67, 122
J.-M. de Forceville (Cedri): 166 below left
M. Foucault (Rapho): 69
J. Fronval: 18, 29, 32, 40, 42 above right, 45, 50 below, 54, 62 below left, 66 below, 68, 74, 77, 112, 114, 118, 144, 146, 164, 166 above right
A. Gaël: 95 above centre and above right, 98 below, 108 below, 140 left
M. Garanger: 28 left, 53
G. Gerster (Rapho): 12, 138
H. Gloaguen (Viva): 13, 167 above
F. Gohier (Pitch): 110
L. Goldman (Rapho): 166 below right
M. Guillard (Top): 120
Hachette (La Cigogne): 7, 33, 47, 49, 59, 64, 119 right, 126, 141
F. Hidalgo: 115, 161, 166 above left

P. Hinous (Top): 10 above and below, 80 below, 135
F. Jalain (Cedri): 85
H. Jeanbrau (Rapho): 133 right
J. Larrier (Rapho): 127
K. Lawson (Rapho): 133 below left
G. Le Querrec (Viva): 82, 84 above left
Loïc-Jahan: 58, 61, 62 above right, 76, 80 above, 81
G. Marineau (Top): 160, 165
S. Marmounier (Cedri): 63, 73 above
J. Martinengo (Fotogram): 124 above
J.-L. Mennesson: 153 above left and below
P.-L. Millet (Top): 131
A. Molinier (Jacana): 72
M. Nahmias: 154 below
M. Nahmias (Top): 66 above, 78, 123
J. Niepce (Rapho): 105, 151
C. Olivier: 75, 111 below, 136
G. Ollive: 84 above right
L. Pélissier: 100, 106, 145
"VU du CIEL par alain perceval": 84 below right, 148
F. Puyplat (Fotogram): 23 above
C. Raimond-Dityvon: 86 right, 87
G. Rebuffat: 70, 71
J.-N. Reichel (Top): 15, 20, 21, 28 right, 51, 98 above, 99 above centre and below left, 158 above, 159
P. Remi (Rapho): 150 right
M. Riboud (Magnum): 117 above left
C. Rives (Cedri): 163
C. Sappa (Cedri): 140 right
S. de Sazo (Rapho): 56, 137
J.-G. Séruzier (Rapho): 52
H.-W. Silvester (Rapho): 35, 39, 41, 42 above left, 89, 91, 113
D. Stanimirovic (Fotogram): 34
P. Tetrel: 14, 25, 93, 94 above left, 95 below left and below right, 96
M. Thersiquel (Fotogram): 132 above
J. Verroust: 8, 9, 22 below, 23 below, 24, 36, 86 left, 99 above right, 128, 155 right, 158 below
G. Viollon (Rapho): 38
S. Weiss (Rapho): 37, 42 below right, 43 above
Yan: 26, 27, 104, 108 above, 109
Yan (Rapho): 101

Layout by Jean-Louis Germain

This book
was printed on 15 July 1977
by the Imprimeries Brodard Graphique, Coulommiers